# Praise for *Taming Your Crocodiles Practices*

"*Taming Your Crocodiles Practices* is a personal tool for all leaders and followers looking to master authenticity and find greater purpose in their daily journey. Imagine the opportunity to explore who we are and what we want to accomplish - without fear. An extension of Hylke Faber's brilliant treatise, Taming Your Crocodiles Practices provides the component tools to unlearn fear-based leadership and practice constructive, creative and inclusive mindsets and behaviors with habit-forming frequency and consistency. A must for those ready to move past lip-service to liberation."

> —Toni Townes-Whitley, President, US Regulated Industries, Microsoft

"How do we know ourselves? Practice! Hylke's newest book offers us seventy-seven thoughtful and accessible practices toward greater self-discovery, creative expression and ever-expanding potential."

> —Chris Ernst, Vice-President, Leadership & Organizational Effectiveness, Workday; author of *Boundary Spanning Leadership*

"*Taming Your Crocodiles Practices: Daily Reflections for Leadership Depth* is a magical combination of deeply wise insights and specific methods to make these insights a reality in your life. I highly recommend this book for any aspiring leader looking to grow professionally but, more importantly, as a person."

> —Matt Oppenheimer, CEO, Remitly

"With great joy I have read this workbook. And it has pleased me to feel the vulnerability of the author, which opens ways for both the reader and the practitioner. Because of the vulnerability and openness of Hylke, he becomes more of a co-passenger than a coach who tells you how it is. Also, I like the fact that you have a choice of exercises related to your personal needs at every given moment. Hylke really connects to the material, which for me is the essence of personal leadership!"

> —Wiet de Bruijn, Partner, Delight Group; former CEO VBK Publishers

"Hylke scores a home run again. *Taming Your Crocodiles Practices: Daily Reflections for Leadership Depth* is a unique and easy-to-read, practical book on personal and professional growth. Hylke reinforces key concepts from his first book, continuously taking the reader out of their comfort zone and posing challenging questions on how to think differently. In addition, by providing daily tips, he helps shape positive habits and behaviors, with a growth mindset, all required to be a great leader. I highly recommend his book for any current or future leader, as well as for a reader in search of a purposeful and meaningful life."
    —Gioji Okuhara, Board Member & CEO, Brazilian consumer
        goods companies

"Through this simple yet powerful and practical book, I continue to explore my fears, or crocodiles, and go deeper in myself. I connect to that place of peace and of a growth mindset. With my busy life and working with world humanitarian crises, this book helps me to be intentional and to continue to practice my growth mindset and find that place of peace. The more I practice leading with my authentic inner self, the more effectively I am able to support leaders I work with globally. These practices apply universally: across different cultures, countries, and religions. I highly recommend using them, wherever you work and wherever you are from."
    —Dr. Valerie Nkamgang Bemo, MD-MPH,
        Deputy Director, Emergency Response
        Global Development, Bill & Melinda Gates Foundation

"A critical part of leadership requires the realization that we must continue to learn and grow. We must find space to tame our fears so we can show our vulnerability, honesty, and share encouragement in an authentic way. I found this space while reading *Taming Your Crocodiles Practices: Daily Reflections for Leadership Depth*. The concept of the crocodile and the owl is very relatable and easy to integrate into a daily practice. I use this as a reminder to stay on the edge of discovery and wonder, which has opened my eyes to infinite possibilities."
    —Marci Marra, Partner, Sia Partners

"*Taming Your Crocodiles Practices* underscores an important point that the academic literature on leadership has largely overlooked—to wit, that the first step a would-be leader must take in the art of leading an organization is knowing thy self. Once you have your own act together, you can start to lead others."
    —Ray Horton, Frank R. Lautenberg Professor of Ethics &
        Corporate Governance at Columbia Business School

"In his new book, *Taming Your Crocodiles Practices: Daily Reflections for Leadership Depth*, Hylke accurately and thoughtfully captures the fundamental development challenge that all humans face: that is to manage our limbic system and to master our fears so that we can uncover our true, loving nature. The practices in this book help us to lead from our heart's wisdom, rather than from our fear-based conditionings."

—Andrew Blum, CEO, The Trium Group

"When you step into a leadership role the weight of responsibility is immediately evident. Among the emotions that confront the moment are thoughts of worthiness and doubt. Embracing the challenge means amplifying your own capacity to explore and understand effective coaching skills that lead teams to success.

*Taming Your Crocodiles Practices: Daily Reflections for Leadership Depth* is a powerful platform to gain skills for reflection, perspective, and growth. Leaders must use these essential tools—not only for their own journey, but also for the people they engage and the organizations they serve. This book presents realistic challenges and powerful questions to help leaders gain depth in creative thinking, purposeful discussions and decision making. Regardless of career stage or job title, this book provides a valuable and essential framework for all professionals."

—Carol Geiger-Wank, alumna, Columbia Business School Executive Education Leader as Coach, senior leader in a governmental agency

"My ninety-year-old Uncle Bill is one of the happiest people I know. He has a modest garage filled with tools he has used throughout his life to make changes, do repairs, or perform maintenance. With the release of *Taming Your Crocodiles Practices*, Hylke Faber has created a perfect sequel to his inspired book, *Taming Your Crocodiles*. He has gifted us an exceptional set of tools and practices to enable key life changes, initiate behavioral repairs, and perform the maintenance on our own lives and relationships, so that we may be better leaders and realize greater humanity in our actions. The seventy-seven daily practices can be used solo, in a duet, or as an ensemble work. They have been lovingly derived via an extraordinary synthesis of his global consulting practice, multi-disciplinary research, the study of music and his learning journeys through Eastern and Western philosophies. Bravo, Hylke!"

—Rebecca Kerr, Founder, Global Creative Solutions Group

"The leader today has already taken many courses in the market. So, what's next? With this practical book, Hylke paves us a path to accelerate our growth through warm and compassionate guidance, and with exercises that we can apply from minute one. He reminds us that true, honest leaders roll up their sleeves practicing and reflecting daily, have a solid base about who they are, and accept and work with their shadows, because it is not about hiding but about taming our crocodiles. This book is such a gift for us!"
> —Bibiana Badenes, PT (physical therapist), rolfing practitioner, somatic coach

"Growing as a person hurts sometimes. In discussion with my crocodiles and looking for my owls daily, I find it very helpful to have this rich portfolio of practices available to me that Hylke shares in his new book. When I'm puzzled how to move on, they help me to see things from a different perspective, or to recognize old patterns in the various aspects of my leadership. Is it my overdrive again, acting too dominant, do I really listen for other people's intentions, and underlying interests, do I give my wisdom enough space? The practical exercises don't ask lots of time or study. Knowing there will always be new crocodiles showing up and owls emerging, I'm pleased to now have this travel guide on my never-ending tough, yet inspiring journey of leadership."
> —Erica Schaper, President, NHL Stenden University of Applied Sciences

"Hylke's new book provides us with a daily dose of self-knowledge. The seventy-seven practices are great for learning something new every day and reflecting on yourself and your business environment. It helps me to be more attentive, to understand human behavior better, to see things more calmly and to find better solutions for big and small problems. It is written in a vivid and humorous way. I especially liked the examples of Crocodile FM and Owl FM as permanent radio stations in our heads. Hylke always asks fascinating questions. One of the most profound questions for me was from practice 7, 'What is most important to me?' I recommend this book to anyone who wants to learn more about themselves and others and feels ready to grow."
> —Mark Schlegel, Director Sales & Marketing, Roxxlyn Design GmbH

# TAMING YOUR CROCODILES PRACTICES

## Daily Reflections for Leadership Depth

## HYLKE FABER

Foreword by René Yoakum
Chief Customer & People Officer, Remitly

ixia
PRESS

Mineola, New York

*Bibliographical Note*

*Taming Your Crocodiles, Practices: Daily Reflections for Leadership Depth*
is a new work, first published by Ixia Press in 2020.

*Library of Congress Cataloging-in-Publication Data*

Names: Faber, Hylke, author.
Title: Taming your crocodiles practices : daily reflections for leadership depth / Hylke Faber.
Description: Mineola : Ixia Press, 2020. | Summary: "How do you learn from the basis of who
  you are rather than from conditioned thinking? How do you turn self-discovery into a daily
  habit? How do you inspire others? Hylke Faber explores these and other questions, offering
  exercises that will deepen your appreciation for the adventure of life and leadership, help
  you connect with your true calling, and turn your fears into growth practices. The essential
  companion to Faber's Nautilus Silver Award-winning Taming Your Crocodiles"— Provided
  by publisher.
Identifiers: LCCN 2019060232 | ISBN 9780486841236 (trade paperback)
Subjects: LCSH: Leadership. | Self-actualization (Psychology)
Classification: LCC HD57.7 .F3293 2020 | DDC 658.4/092—dc23
LC record available at https://lccn.loc.gov/2019060232

Ixia Press
An imprint of Dover Publications, Inc.

Manufactured in the United States by LSC Communications
84123501
www.doverpublications.com/ixiapress

2 4 6 8 10 9 7 5 3 1

2020

For Laverna Dean Oliphant.
You teach me unconditional love.

*"Knowing constancy is insight.*
*Not knowing constancy leads to disaster."*
Lao Tzu, Tao Te Ching, chapter 16

# Contents

# Foreword

*I slept and dreamt that life was **joy**.*
*I awoke and saw that life was **service**.*
*I acted and behold, **service** was **joy**.*

—Rabindranath Tagore

In life, there are two motivating forces: fear and love. At work, many of us translate love into purpose or mission. If you have read (and I highly recommend you do!) Hylke Faber's previous book, *Taming Your Crocodiles,* you are already on the path to growing your leadership impact by consciously managing fear and more authentically serving your customers and teams. Being human, we continue to experience fear in ourselves and through our colleagues, and therefore need ongoing practice and support. That's why I am so excited about the rich resources and exercises in this book, *Taming Your Crocodiles Practices.* I've already added it to my essential personal and professional toolkit. I believe you will, too.

I began working with Hylke in 2011 when I was leading a large, global, customer-facing business at Microsoft. In order to better serve our customers around the world, we wanted to build a culture where our people were customer-first, authentic, and constantly growing their own technical and service skills. Many were coming from a place of fear—fear of their scorecards, fear of making mistakes, fear of going outside perceived boundaries to truly do the right thing for customers. Using StrengthsFinder assessments (Gallup) and Conscious Business principles (Fred Kofman), we began a journey focused on listening, experimenting, and simplifying. With Hylke's help, we quickly learned that while you can intellectually "get" the culture and behaviors, you must EXPERIENCE to internalize and grow. That's where this book will support you with exercises you can work on yourself, with your colleagues, and across your teams.

In 2018, I joined Remitly, a mission-driven fintech startup transforming the lives of immigrants and their families by providing the most trusted financial service products on the planet. Nine months later, I got the opportunity to lead our HR and Recruiting teams, while continuing to manage global Customer Success. Talk about fear! Although I had managed large teams and operational organizations in the past, and strongly believed in our people and their capabilities, I had never worked in, let alone led, HR functions. Could I learn quickly enough to help our teams and business in a high-growth startup environment while continuing to double our growth annually? Hylke, as a trusted advisor and coach, helped me quiet my crocodiles, grow my capacity, and tap into deeper wisdom to support our people, leadership teams, and our customers. Today, I continue to focus on being more present and vulnerable, building from first principles, and living the intersection of our cultural values—all so I can lead authentically and joyfully serve our customers and people. Being able to see and name crocodiles reduces their grip and power and shows me a path to greater love and impact.

We know that leadership is a never-ending journey. Just when you think you've "arrived," a new challenge or opportunity emerges, ancient crocodiles lunge, and the next level of work begins anew. This book is an owl's nest of individual practice and team exercises to extend your growth. I especially like the format where Hylke describes a challenge or mindset as context for the exercise that follows. That approach makes this book a rich and easy-to-use resource for individual and group development. I encourage you to jump in, practice often, and fully experience these practices. Wishing ongoing growth for you and your teams.

RENÉ YOAKUM
*Chief Customer & People Officer*
*Remitly*
*March 2020*

# Introduction

I STARTED PRACTICING self-reflection with Jonelle Reynolds, a deeply loving human being and coach, in 2003. Seventeen years later, I am still working with her. Our work together has become one of my core practices and has led me to discover more of who I truly am and how to be of service in the world. Our conversations have become one ritual that I relish.

One thing I noticed from the beginning about our conversations is that I would invariably leave feeling lighter. In the beginning, I thought it was because we had solved some problem that I had. After a while, I started to realize that it was really me connecting more deeply with myself that made the difference. One question I have heard thousands of times from her is: *"Is that a thought coming from love or fear?"* When I am not sure, I am stuck in fear thinking.

At first, I thought being in fear is how life is. Am I not supposed to be fearful? Slowly it dawned on me that my fears are in fact about me trying to protect some sort of sense of self, my identity, like I should be nice, perfect, or liked. The less attached I am to my identities, the freer I feel, and, paradoxically, the more ready I am to be fully myself and to engage with life, feeling safe and supported.

How to let go of attachment to my identities? That's where the second question comes in. *"Is that true?"* I have also heard this question thousands of times. Is it true that I should be perfect, pleasing, better than, special, fit in, etc.? Is it true that I should act from that fearful place? Letting this question do its work on me, taking truth in, I connect to a sense of inner freedom that is vast. The more I touch this inner space, the more I am able to be truly kind with myself and others and do what I am called to do in my life and work.

This, in four paragraphs, describes the essence of what I have been learning over these past two decades. Every other realization has come from this. I have based my coaching practices on it, written books, and most importantly, set an intention to live and lead more and more from who I truly am, free from fear, full of that for which there are no words. Some call it unconditional love, presence, peace, joy. Others the unborn, the ground, emptiness, sky, life, etc. Words don't quite capture it. They are only pointers to what is true about us.

Realizations about ourselves are sometimes sudden. More often, they are part of a long, winding road. This is where practice comes in and that's why I wrote this book. I noticed in myself and in the people I coach that the more we practice self-reflection, the more we become familiar with our depth and learn to live and lead from it. Especially on the days that seem hard when we don't want to pause and reflect, it's worthwhile to do exactly that. As we have the courage to be deeply honest with ourselves about what's happening, and how our own fear-conditioned minds contribute to whatever challenge we are facing now, the more we become aware of the workings of our inner selves, and the more we are able to make choices to let go of old ways of thinking and behaving and make space for something new. We learn to recognize what we call our *crocodiles*, our fear-based conditionings, and to live and lead from a truer, wiser, and more compassionate place, which we call our *owl*. We learn to tame our crocodiles and bring them under the aegis of our wise and compassionate owl.

This book contains seventy-seven crocodile taming practices. I invite you to explore them. Read them and complete them in the context of your life and work. Imagine what becomes possible for you when you lead from a wiser, more compassionate place, less under the influence of any of your crocodilian conditionings.

I invite you to see yourself as a leader even if you don't have any people on your team. We are always leading ourselves and may be influencing others more than we are aware. The more grounded we become in who we truly are, the more we are able to focus on what we are called to do, whether it is by ourselves or with others. The more we touch our own depth, the more we can bring that to any situation and person that crosses our path.

You can use the book in several ways, including as a day reader. Every day, or every few days, pick a practice that you feel drawn to, spend a few minutes with it and let yourself experience the insights that may come online with your reflection. You may make it part of your morning routine. You can also work with it as a ready-to-meet-now coach. Maybe you read a practice just before a challenging meeting, or just after something challenging has happened. Just spend a few minutes with yourself and let the practices help you remember more of what you are truly about and made of.

The book has eight parts. The first five consist of "Leading Self" practices and the last three are about "Leading Others." You can do the practices in any order, although I recommend you do some of the practices from Part 1 (Exploring Foundational Growth Practices) to get started, especially if you are not yet familiar with this type of work. And even though the first five parts are focused on our relationship with ourselves and the last three on our relationship with others, any practice can be used with either orientation.

Maybe you have read *Taming Your Crocodiles: Unlearn Fear & Become a True Leader*. Then you may find that these practices help you deepen your learnings from that book. If you haven't read it yet, that book may give you further context for the practices described in this one.

Sometimes, doing a practice, you may get a deep insight. At other times, you may not resonate with the practice at all. That's fine. Take what you like and leave the rest. You are the expert on you. You know what's relevant for you now. These practices are about helping you stand more and more in your own two shoes. In the end, no one, no book, no teaching, can tell you what you are about. Only you can.

I chose to include seventy-seven practices because I associate the number seven with completeness and infinity. To me, we are never done practicing or discovering more truth, yet always complete in what we truly are.

I am grateful that you have chosen to join me in this journey to discover more of our truest depths and how to share that with others.

Happy crocodile taming.

# PART 1

## Exploring Foundational Growth Practices

# PRACTICE 1
## From Ego Rat Race to Presence Miracles

"THANK GOODNESS IT'S Friday." "This day is almost over." "I've just got to make it through the day." Have you ever had these kinds of thoughts? It's so easy to miss what is truly magnificent about the now. And that makes sense because our fearful primitive reptilian mind, which we call our crocodile, is only interested in our egoic survival and has us working hard for that, leaving little or no time to rest and smell the roses—deeply appreciating ourselves, our colleagues and our work together. This unique moment that will never come again.

The crocodile has us focus on the survival of our sense of self, such as the Perfect One, the Nice One, the Competent One, the Helpful One, the Rescuer, the Wise One, and the Special One. Each of these identities takes a lot of energy to keep propped up. For me to be perfect, everything has to go according to my plan; to maintain my nice image, I need to manipulate people into liking me; to be competent, I need to always be prepared; to be helpful, I keep scanning for opportunities for what else I should be doing; to be the Rescuer, I surround myself with people I think need saving; as the Wise One, I always need something erudite to say; and as the Special One, I need to live in this special house, in this special town, with this special family, doing this very special work, having this very special position.

When we are trying to keep up our appearances, the costs of doing so are sky high: we exhaust ourselves working toward our image, don't spend time on the people and things we really enjoy, and drain our energy with the constant self-judging of "Am I there yet?" and "Am I good enough?" Now, if the return on this investment were worth it, I would be all for it. But is it? Upon reflection, most of us report that pursuing any of these identities does not provide the lasting happiness, fulfillment, and peace that we are looking for deep down. Even if I have had a perfect day, I worry about what tomorrow will bring.

How can we access a more lasting sense of joy, peace, and fulfillment? When we lose touch with that which is eternal, we keep running after what is not. In my experience, when I attain what I thought I really wanted—for example, approval, a good mate, a happy client, even good health and prosperity—it gives me only a momentary sense of relief or satisfaction, but nothing lasting. Somehow, something in me knows that I need to look a little deeper.

What do we find that is lasting when we look more deeply inside of ourselves? It's hard to describe, even impossible to put words to. I experience it as a sense of presence, of being aware, which has qualities such as clarity, light, care, and peace. Presence has a sky-like quality— it's always there, and encompasses the ever-changing patterns that appear in it. While presence is always here, I don't always experience it. My mind often has me glued to the thoughts of the day, which are mostly about some way of keeping my egoic identity intact. That is not to say that all my thoughts are ego-driven. Thoughts can be very helpful and are necessary to be an effective leader. Yet I know my thoughts have become obsessive when I don't seem to be able to stop thinking them.

To cut through this obsessive crocodilian clutter in my mind, I allow myself a moment of being supremely disinterested in any thoughts and feelings and dedicate myself to something that is constant in my physical body, which is my breath. Resting my attention on the in- and out-breath, I find that my thoughts and feelings tend to calm down and I start to notice the space beyond them—something that doesn't change, that is still, compassionate, always there, constant.

Try it out now. Take a few conscious breaths into your belly and start to rest your attention on the space behind your thoughts and feelings. Notice how vast this space is—infinite really, like the sky. Notice when you access this space from your heart center it has a sense of warmth to it.

What would it be like to approach our day being centered in presence, rather than being taken on an unconscious often-not-so-joyous-ride of the obsessions of the mind? From the space of presence, would we still rush from meeting to meeting, from commitment to commitment, feverishly checking messages in between? Or would we appreciate the time, place, and people we are with now more?

Try it out and step out of the I-have-to-always-be-productive mind-made rat race, and, with the eyes of presence, observe the endless micro-miracles that are unfolding in front of and inside of you. Maybe it's the feeling of your breath in your belly, or the sense of warmth from the sun, or the aliveness you feel being chilly, or the depth of feeling sad or mad. Whatever it is, notice the sky-like presence that you are, encompassing every experience, thought, and feeling. Learn to savor every experience from that space of deep joy that is our birthright.

## Leadership Practice

*How present are you now on a scale from 1 to 10?*

*What would happen if you allowed yourself to become a little bit more present now?*

*Look at something you enjoy—it can be the sky, a flower, your phone, a hand, or whatever strikes your fancy. Look at it first while you're totally distracted, Presence a 1. You are not here. What is your experience like? Now allow your sense of Presence to go closer to 10.*

*How do you experience the object that you are looking at now? How do you experience yourself?*

## PRACTICE 2
## Is this True?

Do you ever wake up at three in the morning to find your mind spinning? Our primitive crocodilian mind's primary objective is to help us survive, and is invested in keeping us in a continuous state of anxiety.

Midnight obsessive thinking is a wonderful strategy to keep us on high alert, thinks the crocodile. Better think through all the options, so you're prepared, it adds.

Looking at this when we are more lucid, we realize that all our obsessive thinking only achieved one thing—it kept us from sleeping and tired us out. Some of us even wake up with obsession hangovers—still feeling groggy from our midnight mental meandering.

Others among us thankfully sleep soundly through the night, but even they get caught in obsessive, unconstructive thinking during the day. How do we break the cycle?

As the crocodile will not easily give up, we will need to apply some effort. We need to be committed to letting go of our obsessive thinking. I have found that a great starting point is by breathing deeply into my belly and resting my attention there for a while. Then I start asking myself some questions that can bring me back to reality.

For example, I might have a thought like, "I won't be able to do this well." I can choose to interrupt this thinking by asking myself a few very simple questions, some of which I learned from wisdom teacher Byron Katie:

- Is this true?
- Is this absolutely true?
- Who would I be without this thought?

Is it true that I may not be able to do this well? Yes, for sure; I don't know whether I have the skills. Then I can ask, "Is it absolutely true that

I may not be able to do this well?" Let me think on this. No thought is absolutely true, because thoughts are only a description of reality and not reality itself. So, all my thoughts by definition are not 100 percent absolutely true. Hmm, this gives me some space.

Then, my favorite question to cut through crocodilian obsessive thinking: Who would I be without this thought? Without this thought I would be free, relaxed, simply here. And I realize I still am not sure whether I will be able to do it, but I feel relaxed about it, and can use some of this relaxed energy to prepare myself, increasing my chances that I actually will succeed. Plus, deep down, I know that I am never just working in a vacuum. I am not alone. Even when my team is not physically with me, there is all of nature, the whole universe that I am part of that is also working through me, just like the sun is working through the tree by giving it sunlight and the river is working through the wolf by quenching its thirst. Somehow the universe provides me with the intuitive insights that help me know how to best be of service.

Stepping out of my obsessive, fear-based crocodilian thinking by questioning it for truth, I also step out of my small-separate-me shell and connect myself to the whole: other people, clients, the universe. Naturally, the question may shift from "Can I do it?" to "How can I be an instrument?" "How can I be of service?" With that orientation, I realize I have nothing real to lose—maybe I will lose parts of my crocodilian ego identity, which is not real anyway. I have only to gain—the experience of giving, of being of service.

In this process, notice how the crocodile calms down and the wiser, more compassionate, and more loving parts—our owl—come to the foreground, not only to take care of us, but also to take care of everyone and everything around us.

## Leadership Practice

*Think about a situation in which you feel stuck in obsessive thinking, and ask yourself these four questions:*

**1.** *Is this true?*

**2.** *Is this absolutely true?*

**3.** *Who would I be without this thought?*

**4.** *How can I truly be of service?*

*Notice what happens with your sense of fulfillment, connection with others, and effectiveness.*

# PRACTICE 3
## Gentle Inquiry

L IFE IS OUR greatest teacher," say the wisdom teachings. This sounds so good, and yet how do we practice this? We tend to make our greatest leaps in consciousness when things are going not so well. We make these shifts when somehow, as if by grace, we make it through these difficult moments and come out on the other side feeling lighter, possibly taller and more powerful on the inside, and more connected to ourselves, others, and the whole of humanity.

Our crocodile is of course not interested in this. All the crocodile wants is safety. Safety first, second, third, and for the rest of your life, says the crocodile, even if it means you will never grow. You at least were safe and protected, coddled in the bosom of certainty, reflects our crocodilian friend.

Fortunately, we as humans also have an innate desire, like the rest of nature, to grow, to evolve, to become who and what we can become. That drive for evolution expresses itself differently for everyone at different times—some work toward becoming excellent in their craft, others focus on finding their next great adventure. Some dedicate themselves to taking care of others, some give their lives to a humanitarian cause and work to make an impact. Other groups work toward beautifying their home, another to being more comfortable and healthy, yet another to growing their financial assets. Some give themselves to cultivating wisdom, compassion, and love. Many of us pursue multiple growth interests in our lives, often at the same time.

If growth is such an integral part of life, how can we make sure it's something we do well, maybe even enjoy? I think of growth as a sculpture-carving project. When Michelangelo was once asked how he made the beautiful statue of David in Florence, he responded, "I saw an angel in the stone and I carved to set it free." Growth requires the dedication and focus of the stone carver. It starts with an understanding of what we believe our "angel" is. I see this as our authentic self, the truth of our being, unconditional love, peace, presence, loving awareness, unlimited potential, that which cannot be put into words. The stones we are removing are our learned crocodilian beliefs and habits, which live in us at many levels, including the physical, intellectual, emotional, and—for lack of a better word—spiritual. True growth is unlearning fear, so that the essence of who we are can come to the foreground. True growth is letting go of all that we are not, all the crocodilian stories we have stored in our nervous system, so that these, like bits of stone carved away, fall off of us, allowing our essence to shine through.

From the vantage point of the angel, we can use literally everything as a mirror to help us see what is true about us and what is not. For example, when we get negative feedback, we may notice our crocodilian reactivity that wants to defend us. Then we can ask, with the gentle energy of the carver: Is it true that I need to defend myself? What part in me requires defending? Upon introspection I may find that the parts in me that believe I need to defend myself are rooted in a fear, such as the fear of me not being worthy or good enough. Then I can contemplate scrubbing this piece of stone from my consciousness. Who would I be without this thought?

This is not inquiring with a sledgehammer. It's a gentle process, like the sculptor carving his piece of art. We can serve our authentic self and the uncovering of it by being inquisitive yet gentle, practicing two core qualities of our essence—wisdom and compassion—as we do our carving work. Deliberately practicing gentleness and inquisitiveness, we get to know more of what we are made of by applying these essential qualities in our journey of self-discovery. How we go about our journey of self-discovery is so important. We get to know our angel by applying an angel-like approach to uncovering it. Then we become the angel uncovering the angel within us. We don't give in to the crocodile, who even has a harsh agenda for our self-discovery process, thinking, "I better get this done now," "I don't want to know what I am made of because I am unworthy," and "I will never get it" or "I need to get there first."

We can apply similar gentle inquisitiveness when things are going well. The crocodile might say, "I did this," "I am special," "I better hold on to this," or "I better show off, so they know I am worthy." We can notice these thoughts and ask ourselves, also in the midst of victory: What is my crocodile afraid of now that it has me be attached to this current favorable outcome?

Chances are that underneath lurks a similar fear of being unworthy. Then we can ask, with gentleness: Is this true? And who would I be without it? Chances are we'll learn to savor our success with far greater humility and deeper joy, allowing ourselves to experience happiness, without the fear of losing it.

---

## Leadership Practice

*Think of a behavior you know is limiting you and yet you find challenging to shift. Being more gentle than you are used to being, ask yourself, Who would I be without this behavior? See what emerges as you let this gentle inquiry do its work on you.*

## PRACTICE 4
### Tapping into the Energy of Self-Discovery
### How Are You Growing?

WHO DO YOU look at first when you see a picture with you in it? Yes, admit it, it's most likely you. We are fascinated by this being that is us. We can use this interest in ourselves both in conditioned crocodilian ways and also from a higher, more expansive place. Are you looking at yourself to see how your hair looked that day, whether you smiled okay, and whether your posture was good? Maybe you were looking at yourself through the crocodilian filter of the judge—evaluating, criticizing, and measuring: "How am I doing?" When we stop and really take it in, we may notice a harsh quality to this orientation. Even when we feel pleased about how we look, it still has the orientation of judgment in it. What will happen when we get sick, are tired, or age? Will we still be able to look ourselves in the mirror then? "How am I doing?" can become a self-punishing orientation for life and leadership.

What if we started to look at ourselves with true self-respect? The word *respect* comes from Latin and also means "seeing again." What if we found the wherewithal to look at ourselves with fresh eyes, and recognized ourselves for who we truly are, beyond all the egoic masks that we learned to put on to help us survive—like the perfect, pleasing, or pathetic one? Then who would we see in the mirror?

The question, "What or who am I?" has been the core question of most wisdom traditions for thousands of years. In ancient Greece "Know Thyself" was even inscribed over the gate to the highly respected and often consulted Oracle in Delphi. Who are we, deep down?

No one can tell us—we can only help each other on our journeys of self-discovery, with questions, by being present to each other and by sharing our own experiences.

Perhaps we see the essence of being human when we look in the eyes of a newborn—something related to love, presence, peace, and joy. I sense we get to use this life, including our work, to grow more and more to get to know our essence and serve from our core. With this orientation, our question may shift from "How am I doing?" to "How am I growing?" How am I growing by seeing more of who I am? How am I growing in expressing that in my work? How am I growing in sharing who I am at home?

Sit with this question, "How am I growing?" for a moment. Notice what comes up for you. You may experience some discomfort, maybe because the question is not yet familiar, and you may also sense some release, some inspiration, even excitement about the being you already are and the being you are becoming. When we make self-discovery a core orientation of our life, we may start to see ourselves and everyone around us as journeys-in-progress, each at our own pace, in our own ways, with our own unique ways of traveling on the path, including our own struggles, pain, confusions, and desires.

With the orientation of "How am I growing?" a challenging business meeting can turn into an exploration of how we can become more honest with ourselves and with others, and how to do so in a respectful, compassionate way that accepts and appreciates others in the room. A while ago, I had a conversation with a publisher who was translating *Taming Your Crocodiles* into another language. The translation they had made so far was not up to my standard. I did share my opinion, and instead of making them wrong about what they had done, which my crocodile would have loved to do, I simply stated my position and inquired into theirs, asking what they thought about the excerpts from the translation I was sharing to illustrate my perspective. What followed was not what my crocodile had expected. My crocodile was ready for a "You are wrong and I am right" type of conversation. Instead, we ended up having a deep and meaningful exchange, where we studied a few lines in the translation intently, and discussed what the translator's motivations for word choice were and what my intentions had been in writing it. In doing so, we found out together why we had a disconnect between the translation and my vision for the book, and we together realized that what we needed to do is to find a different translator whose motivations and preferences were more closely aligned to mine. A potentially explosive conversation turned into a constructive one, in part because I allowed myself to grow past my crocodilian make-wrong tendencies and grow into being and acting with more curiosity and compassion.

Notice that the question "How am I growing?" helps us to stay on the edge of discovery in our life and leadership, enabling us to find new possibilities for action within ourselves that can contribute to more meaningful, collaborative, and effective outcomes. When I am consistently asking myself, "How am I growing?" I can't help but find new sources of wisdom, compassion, and care within me that I can put to good use.

Also, I feel we access a quality of forgiveness by staying oriented toward self-discovery. When I keep asking myself, "How am I growing?" every failure becomes a stepping stone to move forward, every conflict becomes an opportunity to grow in wisdom and compassion, and every criticism becomes a chance to learn more about what is true about ourselves, the other, and the situation. With a growth orientation, every upset becomes a set-up for learning, rather than yet another reason to judge, reject, and punish ourselves.

## Leadership Practice

*"How am I growing?" Practice this question when you face a challenge. See what happens with how you feel and how you relate to the challenge. Then do the same when you experience a windfall, success, or other type of favorable outcome. See what happens with your capacity to be humble and put the uplift to good use, when you stay in the question, "How am I growing?"*

## PRACTICE 5
## Seeing with a Quiet Heart

ITHINK OF my accountant today. Even when it's tax season, and his calendar is booked back-to-back, he tells me he is "not busy." He tells me that with a "not busy" mindset he is able to enjoy the days more, especially around April 15, tax day, and be clearer, more compassionate, and more effective in his work.

My crocodilian mind, hell-bent on survival, wants me to stay busy thinking, with a lot of worry, to keep me on edge, the go-to state for the primitive reptilian nervous system. "Stay on edge," says the crocodile, "at least then I know you'll be ready for the next attack." No wonder we're exhausted by the end of the day, after having listened to another ten hours of "Always More Problems to Fix" on Crocodile-FM self-talk radio.

We always have the option to tune into a different frequency of our consciousness. We call this wiser, more compassionate part our Owl-FM. Listening to this frequency, we likely feel more inspired and refreshed. We have greater bandwidth to address the challenges of our day with resourcefulness, warmth, wit, even joy. How do we set our dial to this energy-giving frequency, especially in the midst of the busyness of our days?

If you are reading this book, you are likely already familiar with many techniques that can help us tune in and tune up, like mindfulness, taking a break, doing some physical exercise, or having a deep, honest conversation with another person. The bad news is that even doing these techniques can keep us stuck at Crocodile-FM. The good news is that we can get ourselves unstuck and shift our inner dial by using a very powerful antenna we all have at our disposal: our heart.

Try this out. Think of an ambition you have. Something you really would like to achieve and/or contribute. It can be a task you have on your to-do list for today, an issue you would like to resolve, or something with a bigger scope, like a dream you have for your life. Whatever it is, please focus your attention on it for a second.

Now take a few deep conscious breaths into your belly and feel your breathing slow down and become deeper. Allow yourself to become present to this moment. Maybe you start feeling a sense of presence, a sense of vibrant stillness, maybe a sense of calm, peace, love, maybe joy. Now start looking at your challenge with the eyes of the heart. Yes, I know this may sound strange. Do it anyway. Imagine there are two eyes painted on your chest. Rest your attention on these eyes and start to feel what it is like to look around you with the eyes of the heart. You may experience a sense of warmth and wonder—maybe appreciation, gratitude, awe. Quite possibly you feel some contraction as well, maybe some fear of being this vulnerable, fear of uncertainty, or a fear of not doing it right. Let all these contractions simply be there. Also look at these contractions with the eyes of the heart. Notice that from the eyes of the heart, the contractions may not seem as painful, urgent, and problematic. From the eyes of the heart, these contractions are simply here. They are part of you, and they are not you. Maybe you sense a degree of trust that these contractions will take care of themselves—there is nothing else to do—simply observe them, and be aware of them from the heart.

Now turn your heart-eyes-attention to the ambition you thought of earlier. What does your ambition look like and feel like from this place? What thoughts come up when you intently focus on your ambition with the eyes of the heart? Maybe you feel a sense of adventure, or discovery. Possibly some warmth toward it and the people involved. It can be that you start seeing more possibilities for action. Or maybe absolutely nothing. Of course, that's fine too. We're just exploring one way to switch our attention to a more heartfelt place—however we access that place. It can be by visualizing a pair of eyes on our heart. Or maybe you access it by gently smiling, and relaxing the muscles in your body a bit more. Or . . . you choose whatever way works for you to access your Owl-FM heart's intelligence.

From the heart, you may feel a sense of life energy running through you. You may experience being part of a greater whole, a sense of being connected to and supported by absolutely everything. While you still will need to put forth effort to realize your ambition, you know you are supported by a quiet power that goes beyond your thinking. Allow yourself to be guided and supported by that quiet heart power.

I know this may sound too esoteric to some of you. Try it out anyway and see what happens when you switch from any habitual worry thinking to seeing people, places, and situations with the eyes of the heart. A stranger may become a friend, a place may turn into a home, and a situation may be your next opportunity for discovery and growth.

I wonder what would happen if we started teaching this question in school: "What does your heart see?" in addition to the more common questions like "What is the correct answer?" and "What do you think about that?" We can train ourselves to use more and more of our body's intelligence—not just the intelligence of the head—to see ourselves and our world from a deeper vantage point.

## Leadership Practice

*Think of a challenge you are facing today. Consider how you will feel, think, and react when you let yourself be guided by fearful crocodilian thinking. What will be the impact of this on your sense of fulfillment, your connection to others, and your effectiveness?*

*Now contrast this crocodilian scenario with living and leading from the heart. What does your challenge look like with the eyes of the heart? Take a moment to breathe deeply and slowly into the belly and rest your attention on your heart center. Once you feel some energy there, imagine there are two eyes on your heart. How do you see your challenge from your heart's eyes? What will be the impact of you heeding this perspective in your response to the challenge on your fulfillment, connection to others, and effectiveness?*

## PRACTICE 6
## The "And" Invitation

Hᴏᴡ ᴄᴀɴ ᴡᴇ be honest *and* respectful? Firm *and* empathetic? Quiet *and* of service? Open *and* decisive? Playful *and* focused? Gentle *and* strong? Self-nurturing *and* caring for others? Staying centered inside *and* willing to stay open to all that's happening in the outside world? Taking our time *and* staying on schedule? Taking care of our finances *and* doing work we love?

Life keeps presenting us with dilemmas, which our fearful crocodilian mind, always in a rush to reach a conclusion now, can only see as "Do you want this *or* that?" This crocodilian reactive chatter keeps us stuck in conflict with ourselves, feeling we have to give up an integral part of ourselves to get what we want now. When we give ourselves the time and attention to look beyond our hasty thinking, we enter a deeper, contemplative space, where we start noticing that we can "conjoin the opposites," as one of my teachers, Adyashanti, likes to say.

To bring the opposites together, we can start by asking ourselves the question, "What if we could be, do, and have both?" We put ourselves on our growth edge. We have to admit to ourselves that we don't yet know how. Putting ourselves at the growth edge feels frightening, an absolute no-no to the reactive crocodilian mind that always wants answers now. Yet another part of us loves the growth edge, like watching a beautiful sunset, or gazing into the stars at night and wondering what lies beyond, being engulfed by the mystery of it all.

Living into the mystery of "what if" is a reward in itself. We wake up in the morning and greet the day as another opportunity for deeper exploration and growth. We put ourselves on our growth edge. Nisargadatta Maharaj wrote this as:

*"Once you realize that the road is the goal*
*and that you are always on the road*
*not to reach the goal, but to enjoy its beauty and wisdom,*
*life ceases to be a task and becomes natural and simple*
*in itself an ecstasy."*

On the road of life and leadership, we greet polarities as paradoxes. The word *paradox* comes from the Greek word *parádoxos*, which literally means "beyond belief." How can I be honest and respectful with this person to whom I have to give tough feedback? Common, crocodilian belief has it that to be respectful I have to keep the other person happy and to be honest I have to sometimes be brutal.

Giving in to these surface beliefs, which we borrow unconsciously from our environment and history, we set ourselves up for anxiety. "But I don't want to hold back," we think. And "I don't want to hurt the other person," says another inner voice. Our anxiety, a telltale sign that we met our next inner conflict, is a sure invitation to look beyond our borrowed beliefs and explore what could be more true than what we have held as true up till then.

Is it true that I have to keep the other person happy? Of course not— their happiness is not our job, it's theirs. The word *respect* literally implies "seeing again." To be truly respectful we can serve the other person by sharing with them what we see, the impact of their behavior on us, and let them come to their own conclusions. We respect their inner knowing —their owl—so much that we will share what we see, not as *the* truth but as *our* truth, and trust that they will take what is helpful and leave the rest. To be truly respectful, we serve the other person with our honest truth, respecting theirs.

If we enter the paradox from the other side, honesty, we notice something similar. The word *honest* comes from the Latin *honestus*, which means "honorable." To be honest with someone, we share our deeper truth with them. To honor ourselves—to be honorable—we need to be in integrity with who we truly are. So who are we that we are to be honorable with? Who are we truly? We can't really put this in words, and yet words like *peace*, *love*, and *joy* seem to touch on something very deep inside each of us.

To be honest with another, we need to come from a peaceful, loving place. This peaceful, loving place cannot but respect the other. So how to be honest *and* respectful? The paradox seems to be an invitation for us to wake up to ways of being more our true selves with another.

We can explore any other paradox in our lives and leadership from the same vantage point. What does this paradox enlighten about my true self? How does this paradox help me discover more of who I truly am and express that in integrity with myself?

---

## Leadership Practice

*See what paradoxes are showing up in your life today. What if both sides of the paradox were true simultaneously? Spend some time contemplating the deeper truth of each half of the paradox.*

*What would it mean if you became truly firm, honest, caring, clear, respectful, or whatever the first word is in your current paradox?*

*Then do the same for the other side of the paradox.*

*Continue the exploration until you have landed at a place of having conjoined the seeming opposites into a new orientation and perspective on who you truly are and how you can be of service from that place.*

# PRACTICE 7
## Living from an Authentic Rather than a Borrowed Perspective

RECENTLY, I WATCHED a rerun of one of my favorite childhood Dutch comedy shows, *Zeg 'ns Aaa* (*Say Aah*), about the lives of a doctor's family. The show aired in the 1980s and about 6 million people in the Netherlands would stay home when it was "on," including my family. I still remember how good it felt to watch this together—big belly laughter, sheer delight, and always some kind of pun at the end. Last night I discovered that the two protagonists had recently passed. That hit me, reminding me that we are always living at death's door. It took me to one of the core questions that has been with me for as long as I can remember: What is most important to me?

Schools, my community, the media, even spiritual books have all fed me answers to this question. At some point I started living my life from these borrowed answers, including "get rich," "be nice," "be the best you can be," "make a difference," "solve some of our biggest puzzles," "enjoy life," and so on. I found that living life from a borrowed answer is inherently unstable—for example, I went after money for a while, until something in me said, "That's not it."

So, what is most important to you? No one can tell us. That's maybe the bad news. The good news is that we each have an inborn inkling what is most important to *us*, just like a seed knows to become a flower, and a sapling knows to become a tree. We each have our unique calling—something that is true for each of us. One coach asked me this: "What is the gift your community cannot afford to lose?" I love this question. For me, it's about helping others realize more of what they're truly made of, their essence, and going deeper and deeper into studying who I am. By touching my own depth, I can help to touch the depth within others, to paraphrase Marianne Williamson.

21

What is most important to you? We may notice that our answers to this question evolve, as we evolve ourselves. As our consciousness expands, we start to see ourselves and others from a broader and deeper perspective. First, we may only perceive our individual selves, leading us to pursue our immediate needs as our life's priority. We may start to become interested in growing out of patterns that no longer serve us, making growth and discovery our priority. And as we do so, we may learn more about our place in the world, and our priority may shift to include serving others. Gradually we may become interested in our place in time, and we start to think about what we want to pass on to future generations and how we want to honor what has been given to us. We may also get fascinated by our place in the universe, and how we are one with all and how we can live and lead from that expanded place.

To me, it's not so much that we have the answer. What gives me energy is to stay in the question," "What is most important to me?" and let the answers come to me as I stay present to what emerges from within. By committing to the question, I grow into my commitment to the most important thing. For example, when I dedicate myself to finding more truth about life and leadership, truth becomes a compass for me. Then the question, "What is most important to me?" becomes a moment-to-moment practice. In this moment, how do I feel called to spend my time and attention?

Contemplating this question deeply, we are called more deeply into this moment. Then we become more open to hear life's nudges—the insights, the revelations—about who we truly are and what we are here to do.

Openness to life teaching us what she wants from us and through us requires dedication. If we let our crocodilian survival thinking take over, we never take the time for these deeper questions and we risk spending our whole lives focused on our survival rather than giving ourselves the permission to truly find out what we are made of. Then we can become like the baby lion who was raised by sheep and therefore started acting like a sheep—until another lion appeared and provided a fresh mirror for the lion-that-had-become-a-sheep to look into and realize that he had been living from a borrowed rather than a true perspective.

Borrowed perspectives are by definition constraining, as we put something on ourselves, like armor, or a costume that doesn't fit us. Staying with a borrowed perspective, we put ourselves in a small box that obscures the vastness, the freedom, the love, the peace that we are.

---

## Leadership Practice

*On a scale from 1 to 10, how much do you live your life from borrowed beliefs about what your life should be about?*

*Now spend some time with the question, "What is most important to me?" and imagine what it will be like to live today more from that question. What new possibilities for fulfillment, relationship, and effectiveness come online with you living more and more from your authentic self?*

# PRACTICE 8
## Being and Working with Pain

A T SOME POINT, I thought that committing to the leadership journey of self-discovery would mean I'd never feel overwhelmed, in pain, or worried again. How mistaken I was! It's as if, because I allow myself to become more aware, I become more sensitive to what's happening, including feeling pain, discomfort, worry, and overwhelm.

How do we work with pain—our own as well as that of others—on our journey of self-discovery and service? Let's first establish what pain really is. We could say it's a sense of discomfort that can be somewhere between mild and intense or overwhelming. Looking closely, we notice that pain is dynamic—it's constantly changing. We may also notice how it is more intense in some parts of our body than others.

Resting our awareness for a moment on that part of the body where the pain is most intense is like putting a hand on someone's shoulder. It can calm the painful feeling, even help it to release and let go. I remember when someone actually put a hand on my shoulder when I was in pain. I instinctively started crying, feeling lighter and more comfortable. It was as if that gesture let my nervous system know that it was safe now to release its hold on this painful energy in my body. We can put our own hand on our pain, by resting our attention gently on the place where it hurts and reminding it that we are here for it, with unconditional love and care.

Giving ourselves permission to be with our pain, not resisting it or judging ourselves for having it (a favorite go-to strategy of our crocodile), can help us to be with the pain from a more conscious, loving place. The word *pain* comes from *poena* in Latin, which first meant "penalty" and later also "pain." Our crocodile tends to make associations between pain and punishment, leading us to think, "Oh, what did I do wrong that has me be in pain now?" Consider how pain-inducing this punishment thinking is. Do we want to give time and attention to this self-judgmental thinking? Is it true that we create our own pain? Of course there are ways in which we can help ourselves to stay out of pain, and yet pain is part of life. We live in physical bodies that age, get sick, and die. If we judge ourselves for having pain, we add a whole other emotionally painful layer to the pain, which may become more painful than the original painful sensation itself.

Looking at pain from our true essence—words like love, peace, and joy point to that—pain becomes something that we learn to embrace, like a child, with love and without judgment. We simply hold it. We may ask it a question, like, "Where does it hurt, my love?" and try to give it some comfort. Being with our pain like a loving parent with an innocent child, we may also learn something from the pain. Maybe the pain is pointing to an unfulfilled need or longing we have. We can gently inquire into what it may be about, and how we can give the child inside what it really needs, in a healthy way.

I learned this week that a partner I work with often wants to change the scope of our work together, which will require me to do a lot more work. My first crocodilian reaction was, "Ouch, I don't need this, I don't have time for this!" I wanted to restore the situation as quickly as possible to the way it was before. I brought an inner "no" to the situation. My mind started spinning how I could manipulate the partner into changing his mind.

Who was talking? Clearly my crocodile. And as I watched this inner self-talk go on for a while, I noticed how a painful situation went from bad to worse. That's how the crocodile works with pain. It doesn't want it; it wants it to go away now and will either overreact, by trying to change the other person or situation, or underreact, by denying the pain—something my crocodile also does often. When I feel pain, and my crocodilian identity of my "being too wise to feel pain" gets activated, I will meditate, smile, or overwork myself, hoping I can push the pain out. When my partner notices I am in pain and asks how I am feeling, my being-oh-so-spiritual crocodile will say, "Oh, I am great," to which he will respond simply by saying, "Mmm mmm...," for me a sure sign that I am in some sort of crocodilian denial.

Pain can trigger a third reaction in me besides overreacting and lashing out or underreacting and denying: that is, dwelling on the pain. My crocodile thinks, "Great, I have all these self-inquiry tools now, let me spend the rest of the morning analyzing this pain," leading me to not take care of other areas of my life and work, and in the end only leading to more pain—the pain of trying to control the pain by analyzing it, another, subtler form of resisting the pain. Anything we resist in ourselves creates an inner barricade that blocks our life energy, which, just like our blood, wants to flow freely through our system and clean and nourish us. Blocking our life energy by resisting pain is painful in and of itself, just like holding our breaths for too long.

How can we work consciously with pain? There is no recipe, just like there is no recipe for raising children. Yet we can choose to be with the pain, from the wisest, most compassionate, most gentle place we can access in the moment of feeling the pain, and let that place in us—that centered orientation—guide us to how to be with the discomfort now. At some point we may want to have a conversation with the pain, asking it, "What do you need now?" Another moment, we may want to just spend a moment breathing with it. And we may also just notice it, like having a child in pain sitting next to us on the passenger seat of our consciousness, while we stay in the driver's seat, taking care of what is needed now in our lives and leadership.

## Leadership Practice

*Notice any pain you have in your body now. Take an inventory of your crocodilian reactions. How are you trying to control and fix situations and other people to get rid of the pain? How are you suppressing it, denying it, telling yourself it's not there? How are you dwelling on it, obsessively trying to get to an answer of "Why?" and "Why me?"*

*Take a moment and imagine what it would be like to be without any of these three crocodilian pain resistance strategies. How can you be with your pain, from a place of nonresistance? How can you live and lead differently today, even when you feel pain?*

# PRACTICE 9
## Becoming the Joyous Welcome

WHAT GIVES YOU joy? Maybe it's achieving a goal, drinking a cup of coffee, receiving recognition, or maybe it's simply the joy of being alive. What would it be like if we could experience joy all the time, even in the midst of challenge, loss, and pain? We're not speaking here about the joy that has its opposite in other emotions. This is about a quiet contentment within us that welcomes everything, no matter how easy, pleasurable, difficult, or painful.

The word *joy* is related to *rejoir*, which also means "to welcome." Joy in this sense is more about an attitude than an outcome. We can choose to welcome everything with an attitude of joy that includes appreciation, gratitude, and curiosity. This may sound impossible to do. What about the injustices we come across at work? What if someone is giving us tough feedback? What if a project we're working on is not going well? How can we be in joy then? And do we want to be?

The crocodilian survival consciousness has a very small idea of what joy looks like. When things are going well for me, I am happy, and when they don't, I am not, and I will immediately go on the defensive to make sure that things go well for me again. Crocodiles find joy in getting what they want, even if it means getting it at the expense of others. In the end the crocodile is *only* interested in our own survival, and our own perspective. However, getting joy at the expense of others only feels good until we develop the capacity to empathize. Then our selfish joy quickly turns into pain, as we feel the pain we inflict on others. It's hard to enjoy our promotion, if we got it at the expense of our teammates. It's hard to enjoy a meal next to a person who is hungry. It's hard to completely enjoy our luxuries when we really connect with the homeless people on our streets.

Of course, there is nothing wrong with deriving joy from getting what we want. The only unfortunate thing is that this conditional joy that depends on outcomes never lasts. We get the job we want and then we lose it. We get the promotion and then we get overwhelmed by work. We become famous and then someone ridicules us in public. We get the big house and as we age, we start to worry about having to get rid of all the stuff we filled it with. We reach one objective and we are already striving toward the next one. Basing our lives on "getting" is a very unstable proposition.

Even "getting" certain positive emotional states is temporary. We feel good and then we feel sad, or anxious; we feel rested and then we get tired; we were calm and now we feel restless. The world of external things, including our own emotional states, cannot provide us lasting joy. That's the bad news.

There is also good news. Sages throughout time have spoken about the Joy of Being: being here now, present, welcoming all experiences as transitory. One way we can connect to this ground of our being, and experience its peace, joy, and love, is by letting go of all our expectations of what should be and what should have happened. Free from expectations, we experience joy. In that sense, expectation is the opposite of joy.

Without the expectation of what *should* be, we are being with what is here now. And as we allow ourselves to more and more deeply be with what is here now and surrender to this moment, we access something eternal, something essential within us that is not tied to any experience or outcome. It has no expectation. It simply *is*. From this simple place of being, we welcome everything. Then we become the host who welcomes every experience as a guest. There is such a joy in welcoming someone and really meaning it. As we welcome all our experiences, we extend the joyful welcome of being who we are. Being unconditionally welcoming is being unconditionally joyful: joyful no matter what.

Now this doesn't mean that welcoming everything means we don't stand up for things, or that we never disagree or make a point. It also doesn't mean we never feel anxious, sad, tired, or angry. On the contrary. We bring our essence, our welcome, to our point of view, to our disagreement, to our emotional state. As we do, we may experience a sense of centeredness, a sense of being rooted in our essence, our heart that gives us strength to welcome everything, as it welcomes us. By opening our heart to everything, we experience the joy of an open heart. We can bring that quality of being to everything, whether we are agreeing or disagreeing, liking or disliking, joining or leaving, feeling happy or sad.

Think about this for a moment. What if I brought my welcoming heart to my next challenging meeting? To the next performance review? Or when I need to fire someone? Or when I am speaking to that new prospect? Or when I need to take an unpopular stance? Then what becomes possible for me? What quiet, joyous strength am I accessing? How can I share that part of my essence with others?

Grounded in the joy of our being, we become an invitation that welcomes all experiences. And being grounded in this open-hearted welcome gives us the energy to engage fully with everything and everyone that we come in contact with.

------

## Leadership Practice

*The opposite of unconditional joy is expectation, not sadness or unhappiness. Make a list of the top five expectations that are keeping your mind busy. For each of them ask yourself: Who would I be without this expectation?*

*Having contemplated this question, freeing yourself from the mind-made expectations, what do you feel without these expectations? How can you be of service to what is needed in this moment without these expectations?*

*How are you growing in getting to know one aspect of your being—unconditional joy?*

## PRACTICE 10
### Owning Our Commitment

WHAT ARE YOU committed to? What do you give your life's energy to? How do you spend your time and attention, the two most valuable assets we have?

Consider a time you were truly committed to something. How did it feel? What did you experience? Chances are you felt focused, alive, content, maybe somewhat fiery, even passionate. Committing ourselves, wholeheartedly choosing something, gives us the freedom to fully engage ourselves, to not hold back, and to work with any obstacles we encounter as steps along the way. We keep going, no matter what. We are not held back by doubt, distraction, or timidity.

The word *commitment* stems from Latin *com-mittere*, which literally means "to give over." We give ourselves over to something else. This can feel both exhilarating and scary. I really want this, and yet, am I sure about this? There are so many times we make a commitment in life and leadership. We choose to take on a job, we choose a spouse, we commit to taking care of our children, we commit to being on time. Life consists of a series of commitments.

This can get very confusing, as our fearful crocodilian mind wants us to commit to anything and anyone that will keep us safe and in control. Don't leave what you know, the crocodile states, stay in your current patterns, however unhealthy or ineffective they may be. Repeat the same story over and over and over again, then you'll be safe. Stay committed to your old identities of not being enough, being weak, being the best, having to please everyone, needing to be the one who understands, the special one and the wise one who counsels everyone else, and the one who is his financial net worth.

Having lived with our unconscious crocodilian commitments for a while, it becomes challenging to get out of them, just like it is challenging to file for divorce, leave a relationship that no longer serves us, or break an addiction. And why would we want to get out of our crocodilian commitments, if we don't sense any real alternative?

Our society is in large part built on fear-based crocodilian commitments of only looking out for our egoic survival at the expense of everyone else, the planet, and our true integrity. Because this societal crocodilian momentum is so strong, it takes an even stronger resolve to live and lead from a different place. Instead of giving our lives, our time, and our attention to whatever societal consensus conditioning prescribes, we make a choice to give our lives to what we truly want.

So, what do we in our heart of hearts truly long for? Once we know that, once we have clarity about that, we become ready to make a conscious commitment that more faithfully reflects who we are and what we really want. No one can tell us what the most important thing is for us. Only we can discover and decide that for ourselves.

"What is most important to you?" is not a question we get habitually asked in our society. That's why our first commitment can be to uncover our deeper commitment, by dedicating ourselves to this question we also explored in Practice #7: What is most important to me?

Death can be a great counselor in this. Reflecting on the question, "When I die, what would I like my life to have been about?" can help us get in touch with our most important thing—that which we want to commit to. Birth is another great teacher. When you look at your baby picture, what do you see in the eyes of that little being? What was this being about? How are you still about this?

So much has been written about what the purpose of life is. We can parrot these writings or we can truly go on a search to reclaim ourselves: What is the most important thing for me?

We know we have come closer to our most important thing when we feel a sense of peace and resolve emerging in us. When we meet our most important thing, we tend to feel joy and freedom, ready to consciously commit ourselves to it. Uncovering our most important thing, we start to sense the freedom of letting go of the crocodilian commitments we have burdened ourselves with.

I am still working on this question. In fact, I have made it my core commitment to keep working with this question of self-discovery. From this initial commitment, I am starting to discover a second commitment that is building in me: to truly love and be of service.

We could say commitments are like a tree. From the seed of one commitment—in my case, to self-discovery—grows a whole organism of other commitments—in my case, also the commitment to truly love and be of service. It's important to be conscious what seed we plant at the root, because from that will grow all our other commitments.

Deeply giving ourselves to our authentic commitments helps to undo our unconscious crocodilian commitments. When our crocodile tries to seduce us to go back to what we know so well, our fear-based ways of being and behaving, we now more deeply know that we have a choice. We can choose to go back into fear, or we can choose to honor our authentic commitment.

This is not a one-time choice. The crocodile keeps feeding us its seductive fear-based tales. Come back here, it says, it's safe and comfortable here and you'll get what you want. Being committed to another way, I respond: "Thanks, but no thanks, I am committed to discovering my true self, and being the love I am discovering that I am."

## Leadership Practice

*Do you ever find yourself avoiding making a conscious commitment? What unconscious commitment are you leaving in place? What is the impact of you staying in your unconscious commitment?*

*Now take some time to reflect on this question: What is the most important thing for you? What is the core seed you wish to base your life and leadership on? Maybe it's already clear to you.*

*It also can take some time. Take a walk with this question, "What is most important to me?" and see what emerges.*

*As you start finding more clarity, start considering how you could base more of your choices today on your most important thing.*

# PART 2

Living and Growing from Intention

---

# PRACTICE 11
## A Three-Part Meta-Intention

WITH A STRONG intention, we free ourselves from crocodilian conditioning that keeps us off balance, and start to uncover our true compass—a life and leadership orientation that is grounded in the truth of who we are, not what our crocodile tells us we should be. Grounded in our meta-intention to come from our authentic core, we start to experience the truth of who we are more and more and connect with the flow of life coming through us. I call this intention to be ourselves our meta-intention as it becomes the root of our other intentions.

We can see our meta-intention to be authentic as consisting of three parts: *connecting* with the ground of our being, *thinking and acting* in integrity with that ground, and *sharing* the gifts that emerge from our ground with our community. *Presence, integrity, and service* are three components of our meta-intention to be our true selves.

For the first part of our meta-intention, notice what happens when you give your full attention to the ground of your being, the presence, the stillness inside of you. You may notice a sense of calm, and maybe also some nervousness or anxiety about letting go of giving attention to thoughts and feelings. As you are allowing yourself to drop deeper into your being, you may notice a space beyond the thoughts and feelings that is like the sky, holding everything, yet not opposing anything and always being there. As you give more time and attention to the sky, you may notice that it starts to meet you—and over time, you become what you give your attention to. Spend some time with this, really allowing yourself to surrender, to give your time and attention to the essence of your being. See how good that feels, how spacious, peaceful, joyous, clear, and warm. When we set out to meet life, life meets us.

You could say the universal human calling, the intention we all share, is to be who we truly are. In simple words, you could say that we all share a calling to be present, to be here now, to surrender and experience who we truly are.

Yet our intention is incomplete when we stop there. Beyond the stillness inside of us, for which we have no words, we are also human beings who act and interact. Therein lies the second part of our intention—living in integrity with our essence. What is the highest truth you have realized? How can you live from this place, especially when you are challenged? Notice what happens when you give yourself fully to living your essence. What about when you are feeling a difficult emotion, like anger, anxiety, or sadness? It may turn into an opportunity to be patient with yourself and stay open to what your feelings are trying to tell you. What happens with a tough conversation? It may become an opportunity to extend your essence, maybe by being truthful, compassionate, understanding, and caring. What becomes of a heavy workload? This too may become a way for you to extend your essence, by surrounding yourself and others with an atmosphere of calm and care, being clear about what is needed now and what is not. And how do you work with the suffering of the world around you? It may turn into a way to extend yourself to others with care, compassion, and clarity.

When we give ourselves to the adventure of living our highest truth, every upset becomes a setup to practice our highest values. Thus, the reward in every challenge is that we get to experience our essence in action, thereby getting to know our true selves even more.

How would we find out about our true wisdom if we never had to face a dilemma? How would we learn about compassion if we never experienced pain; our own or that of others? How would we learn honesty if we never experienced the discomfort of dishonesty? Our work and leadership can be seen as a continuing practice of getting to know who we truly are. When we give of ourselves, we meet ourselves.

The third part of our meta-intention to be authentic is to be of service. Think about how much we learn when we give to someone else. Preparing a meal for another, we learn hospitality, serving their needs. Giving a listening ear, we learn to be open and humble. Being present to someone's suffering, we learn to empathize. When our yearning to serve meets the needs of our environment, we discover gifts that lie inside of us.

---

## Leadership Practice

*Take some time to journal and gradually let an authentic intention in three parts emerge from your writings. Use the prompts below to guide you.*

### Presence:

*Take a few long deep breaths in the belly and let your attention rest on the space beyond your thoughts, feelings, and sensations. Give yourself to this space and see how it meets you with a sense of presence, stillness, love, and peace. Notice that this space is also there when you are having pain or face other difficulty. Allow yourself to rest in the stillness of your being.*

*Write some words that can remind you what your true essence is all about and how you might connect with it later on.*

### Integrity:

*Also consider, being present, what is the highest truth you have realized about who you truly are? What are you truly made of? How can you express this as a leader, with what values?*

### Service:

*And finally, how do you feel called to be of service?*

*What needs do you see within and around you? This could be a physical, financial, spiritual, and/or emotional need you have; the needs of your friends, family, and colleagues; and/or the needs of your community and the broader world.*


*In what forms could your calling meet the needs you see within and around you?*

# PRACTICE 12
## Setting Our Compass: The Ground of Our Being

B EING OURSELVES IS an endless journey. Every day we get to start anew, having new experiences that we can use to get to know and express our true selves. And with all our crocodiles vying for our attention, it's easy to get lost, to forget where we're going, and to get stuck pursuing some egoic identity, like being perfect, pleasing, or know-it-all, at the expense of our true identity.

To not get as easily lost, I find it helpful to do a morning practice where I remind myself of my true being, like looking at a picture of the top of the mountain I am scaling, telling myself, "This is where you are going; don't let yourself get distracted by anything else." This may sound good and also daunting. How do I know I am looking at the right picture? How do I know my fearful crocodilian mind isn't projecting some kind of imaginary goal it would have me waste my time and attention on?

No one can tell us who we truly are. And yet we can use everything, literally everything, to point us to our true essence. Simply contemplate: In all that you experience, what is the one thing that is always here? You may notice that everything we perceive is always changing—the people around us, our belongings, projects, jobs, even our own mental and emotional states. All of it is changing. So, what is constant, that we can always rely on, can come back to, no matter what? What is indestructible, unconditionally here, always?

Our breath is a guide that can take us part of the way to help us see what is always here. Our breath is a symbol of constancy, as it's always with us, at least for as long as we live. Rest your attention for a few moments on the breath; feel the breathing in your lower belly, the gravitational center of your body; and allow yourself to relax a little bit more deeply. Allow the thoughts and feelings to pass through you and allow yourself to drop deeper and deeper into the core of your being, simply by following the inhale and exhale. Notice there is a space at the end of the exhale, just before your inhale starts up again. Allow yourself to drop into that space, like you let yourself fall, and then when the breath starts up anew, place your attention lightly on the breathing again. Keep repeating this: Place your attention on the breath, then on the space in between, then the breath, then the space in between. Start noticing how the breathing is slowing down and the space in between becomes wider. Allow yourself to fall into this space, even start resting in it.

There are no words for this space, and you may notice it's always there, even when the thinking and the feeling starts up again. This space is like the sky that holds everything and doesn't reject anything. It's unconditionally accepting all that is. As the great silence, it has no agenda. It is simply there. This is not the silence as opposed to sound. This is the silence that includes sound.

We can learn to relate to this silent space by accessing it with different perception centers in our body. Relating to the space in different ways is like looking at that picture of the top of our mountain from different angles, so that we get to know it really well. The first angle we take is the perspective from our lower belly. Let's connect with this space from our lower belly now. Allow your attention to really rest on your lower belly and notice how it connects with the spacious silence. You may notice a sense of stillness, of rootedness, of depth. From the belly, the core of our physical being, we tend to perceive the silence of our being as something rock solid, yet also permeable like water, without boundaries. Take note of whatever you're experiencing through the belly perception center of the silence. Next time you enter a potentially destabilizing situation, you may remember your true essence as unmovable, yet moving and including everything, like the sky. Allow yourself to rest as that silent sky.

Now move your attention up to your chest and your heart center. Connect with the eyes of the heart to the great silence, simply by allowing yourself to be still and by placing your attention on the heart center and observing how it senses the silence. You may observe a sense of presence, of warmth, of connectedness, maybe a sense of deep caring, gratitude, and awe, and other sensations. Take note of what you are experiencing.

Your words may become reminders to help you open your heart the next time you feel like closing it. Opening the heart takes courage. It's an act of bravery to open the heart to let yourself deeply feel all that is happening within and around you. Let your attention linger a moment longer in the heart and let the sense of presence embrace you.

Finally, move your attention to the place between your eyebrows, and look from that intuitive sensing center into the depth of your being, the silence that you are. Allow yourself to become really still and look with soft eyes into the silence of being, the space that lies beyond our thoughts, feelings, and sensations and includes all of it. The space that is always here and now. From this place, you may experience the silence as a sense of clarity, being able to discern clearly true from not true, wisdom from hallucination. Take note of your experience of the great silence from this so-called "third eye." The next time you meet a dilemma, you may look at it again with the third eye rooted in silence, seeing clearly what is and what is not.

Indestructible ground, presence, clarity—allow yourself to rest a few moments contemplating these words and the great silence of our essence that they represent. What becomes possible for you when you give your time and attention more intentionally to the ground of your being? How would you lead differently and become more and more connected to your true essence?

---

## Leadership Practice

*Take a few moments to breathe deeply into your belly. Notice any thoughts, feelings, and sensations and let them pass through you. Relax your awareness around them.*

*Then start resting in the awareness, the space beyond all thoughts, feelings, and sensations. Really allow yourself to fall into the silence of your being. Let it nourish you.*

*To familiarize yourself even more with your essence, start resting your attention on your belly and gaze from there into the silence. Then slowly shift your attention to your heart center—look into the silence from the eyes of the heart. Finally, let your attention travel up to your third eye (the area between the eyebrows) and dive into the silence from there.*

*Now drop all sense of practice and simply be here now. Notice what comes online in you as you allow yourself to be connected to who you truly are.*

# PRACTICE 13
## Seven Owl Intentions

THE ENERGY WITH which we approach each moment defines to a large extent our experience of that moment, and our ability to impact and connect with others. If we show up judging someone else, we likely won't connect with them. If we are worried, we tend to be less creative and wise. If we are self-absorbed, we tend to be less empathic and compassionate.

Check in with yourself for a moment. What is the energy you bring to this moment reading these words? What would happen with your experience if you brought even more of your true self to this experience, a sense of presence, peace, unconditional love? Then how would you relate to your experience reading these words now?

Intention comes from the Latin word *intentio*, which means, besides "purpose," also "stretch." Being intentional, we step out of the crocodilian comfort zone of small-minded thinking and we venture into a more expanded way of being. Being intentional requires us to stretch, stepping out of the crocodilian, fear-based autopilot thinking, and to connect with who we truly intend to be. Being intentional means we're making a deliberate choice to be and do what our crocodile doesn't want us to be and do, and to be and do what our essence guides us to be and do, so we can be and act from a place of authentic integrity.

To help us with the intentions we set each moment, each day, and for each challenge, I find it helpful to remind myself of the various sets of choices I have in setting my intentions to be authentic. My go-to intention may not be what I need today. I and others may be better served by my leading and living from a different intention that stretches me more and that is more conducive to taking good care of this moment.

Studying the various intentions we can have, we may discover some patterns. This may provide a window into alternative intentions we may

45

want to stretch into. I found that it's helpful to group our intentions into seven owl intentions that loosely reflect Maslow's hierarchy of needs. The owl stands for the wise and compassionate part of our being. If you happen to be familiar with the chakra system from the East, you may also discover the correlation between the chakras and the seven owls.

I remember them with the acronym "SUCCESS":

1.  *Samurai*—having the warrior-like courage and fortitude to take care of my basic needs, and face my challenges resourcefully without being overwhelmed by them

2.  *Uniting*—creating authentic, empathetic relationships that welcome everyone and go beyond tribal us-vs.-them dynamics

3.  *Centered in purpose*—being driven by my inner compass, pursuing my goals wholeheartedly and with focus, and seeing every "failure" as part of moving forward

4.  *Curious*—opening my heart to life's teachings—the whispers—no matter what, and seeing every moment as an opportunity for discovery, bigger vision, and being innovative

5.  *Extending*—expressing my gift to others unapologetically and caringly

6.  *Sensing*—using intuition, looking for the connection between everything and everyone, integrating the seeming polarities in life, creating cohesion

7.  *Simple*—seeing what is needed and doing it, letting go of all ego personas, simply being and contributing who I am

Take a look—Which owl intention resonates more with you? Which one may be a stretch for you today? Which one do you think is most helpful in your doing what is needed today? There is no right answer. You may find that your chosen intention for today is one that reflects any one of these seven owls, or a combination or variation on it, or something else. It doesn't matter what you choose. It matters *that* you choose.

For a moment reflect on what will become possible for you if you start living this intention times two, maybe even times three or five.

In the next seven practices, we'll spend time with each of the seven owl intentions separately, so we'll get to know them more deeply.

---

## Leadership Practice

*Reflect on the seven owl intentions. Which one will you practice today? How may your being intentional impact your sense of fulfillment, your relationships and your effectiveness?*

*Also notice: How does the crocodile try to derail you? How can you take care of this crocodile, a younger, fearful part of your consciousness, with the loving attention of the owl?*

# PRACTICE 14
## Take Your Samurai Seat (Owl Intention #1)

I AM RUNNING around like a headless chicken," "I'm so overwhelmed, I don't know where to start," and "I feel like I am being pulled in so many directions," we say to ourselves, trying to keep up with the seemingly ever-increasing pace of life. As we get more to do, our mind can start spinning, leaving us feeling restless, ineffective, and disconnected from ourselves and others.

Our body is a powerful tool to help us to get back to sanity. Being stressed, we may feel contraction in our shoulders and heads. This gives a clue to greater relaxation: simply drop the energy back into the lower parts of our bodies, all the way down to our sits bones (pelvic bones) and feet.

Take a moment and notice what it feels like to truly take your seat. Feel your sits bones rest more and more deeply into your chair and sit upright if you can, in a relaxed way. Don't worry about getting it right, simply allow yourself to rest more deeply into your seat. You may start to feel more grounded, maybe even energized from the ground up, like you are connecting yourself into the socket of the earth. You may also experience some discomfort, like anxiety or other forms of resistance to resting in your seat, into this present moment.

The crocodile finds this very scary—it does not want us to take our seat too deeply. It thinks, "I need to be ready for fight or flight at a moment's notice. Truly being here now is very dangerous. Not something I am willing to sign up for." Taking our seat may feel like taking the hot seat for our crocodile. "I'd rather not face reality. That is way too uncomfortable for me. I don't want to discover I was mistaken or contributed to my negative experience in some way. I prefer my story about reality over reality itself," says our crocodile.

Rooted into the seat of who we truly are, we meet life face-to-face. We don't shy away from it. We dare to see it as it is, not as our crocodilian fantasies and nightmares make it out to be. We look our life directly in the eye. We don't flinch. And we feel safe, as we are sitting on the throne of our life.

Sitting firmly in our seat, we see challenges for what they are—opportunities to learn from and contribute to life. Not letting an ounce of our time and attention slip away, we devote it all to this moment. As we dedicate our time and attention to this moment, including its challenges, a sense of rootedness and resourcefulness comes online in us.

The moment we start chasing our crocodiles, we lose power. If we face a financial challenge, and give in to the crocodile's worries about whether we'll ever make it, we are no longer in the seat of the here and now. The more we take this seat of the here and now, the more we stretch ourselves to take care of whatever challenge we have with whatever resources we have now. Then, a financial challenge becomes an invitation for us to tap into our resourcefulness and inner stability.

When we are no longer worrying and fantasizing, we devote our time and attention to what is here now. We start to feel more resourceful and stable when we make an intention to stay rooted in our own resourcefulness and stability. The word Samurai, from Japanese, can evoke this intention to stay rooted and serve from this grounded place no matter what. "Samurai" is related to the Chinese word "*bushi*" which also means "to wait upon." Taking our seat, we take care of, we wait upon life, and we do what is needed.

Ask yourself, on a scale from 1 to 10, how committed are you to taking your seat in your life? What would happen if you increased your commitment, even became warrior-like about it? To face our feisty crocodiles, we need this kind of fierce commitment to deal with them, to see through the hallucinatory stories they keep feeding us.

When we are firmly committed to staying in our own seat, our entanglements with drama (both that of our own crocodiles and that of other people's) loosen. As opposed to being lured by the thrill of yet another episode of "I or you are not good enough," I bring my attention to my seat, first my physical one and then also my energetic one. This allows me to be fully present in the here and now and truly take care of what is needed now, as opposed to pursuing the latest crocodilian fantasy.

---

## Leadership Practice

*Find a place where you can comfortably sit still for a few minutes. Allow your attention to start resting on the breath in your belly and start noticing your sits bones touching what you sit on. Allow yourself to sink more deeply into your seat, while staying upright if possible. Relax downwardly and upwardly at the same time.*

*Allow yourself to receive the nourishment of sitting still. You may experience a sense of stability—maybe also creativity and inspiration. Now imagine someone you are working with. In what ways can you apply this energy of stability and resourcefulness to what you are working on together?*

# PRACTICE 15
## Awake Relationship (Owl Intention #2)

WE ARE CONSTANTLY relating to others. Whether we are with or just thinking about them, we're always with others. Some of my most beautiful and also some of my hardest moments in life have been with others. Relating to others, I have experienced deep connection, a feeling of being understood, intimacy, deep laughter, an opportunity to be of service, comfort and comforting, being held and holding, and lots and lots of learning. I have also experienced being rejected and rejecting, feeling judged and judging, being controlled and controlling, being pleased and pleasing, being blamed and blaming, and being ridiculed and ridiculing. Interacting with others provides us a seemingly never-ending stream of experiences.

Our crocodile, with its sole focus on our survival, sees others simply as a means to an end, or as an obstacle. "How will you keep me safe or help me get ahead?" thinks the crocodile, or "How might you get me in trouble?" Relationships are a great way to get to know our crocodiles well. Crocodiles want us to be dishonest, disrespectful, pleasing, controlling, manipulative, a martyr, a rescuer, more than, less than, or any other flavor of egoic identity-supporting behavior, in relationship with others. Any interaction with another, even just thinking about them, can activate one of our crocodilian patterns.

As we notice these crocodilian patterns, we can pause and choose a wiser and more compassionate response that is not coming from fear, but from peace, love, and joy—aspects of our owl, our true being. The more often we choose our owl, the more likely it is that our crocodiles will get the message and start to relax—often one crocodilian pattern at a time. One caveat though—many of our crocodiles are stubborn; they don't give up so easily. We need to continuously reassure them, just like little children, that it's okay to let go of control of our lives and our relationships.

When we let go of our crocodiles, a space opens up in us and we reconnect with the presence, the peace, the stillness in us. From this present, still place we can't help but notice our relatedness, how we're all part of the same space, the same universe, the same energy. We are deeply related to all our fellow human beings, who just like us are trying to be happy, and who just like us have challenges and crocodiles to work with.

Seeing others as just like us is a radical act for the crocodile. From fear, we can only see the other as something separate from us we need to take advantage of, worry about, or ignore. From love, we see the other is just like us, and we can't help but to want to care for them. We are innately wired to care for each other. If a person collapses on the sidewalk, many of us will rush in to help them, whether they are a stranger or a friend. If a person sitting next to us starts sneezing, we want to offer them a tissue. If a child is about to eat something toxic, we'll help them to put it down, whether it's "our" child or not.

Work conversations are a great way to practice our innate care for each other. The word *conversation* comes from *conversatio*, which means to "turn together." A great conversation is one where both people change a bit on the inside, maybe feel a bit taller on the inside upon leaving it—having been expanded by caring for the other and learning something, by being touched by the other person's care and appreciation, and maybe by having come to a deeper mutual understanding. Or maybe we really enjoyed the conversation, and leave feeling "lit up" inside.

There is no magic formula to caring for others. Yet it helps to consciously decide to relate to the other from our true selves, the peace, joy, love that we are, rather than from our fearful, contracted, self-protecting crocodile who keeps projecting expectations on to others about what they should or should not be to us.

From my true self, I see the other as myself. From my true self, I feel compelled to share honestly with the other what I see. From my true self, I want to honor where the other is, respecting their thoughts and feelings. And from my true self, I sense intuitively when to speak, what to say, and when to listen. From my true self, I sense what the other person really means, feels, and needs. And from my true self, I am clear about what boundaries are wise to keep both people healthy. The list goes on; there is so much to practice and discover in relationships.

———————

## Leadership Practice

*Think of a person you interact with often and ask yourself: How is my fearful crocodile trying to get something from them? Protect me from them?*

*How could I relate to them more from my owl, honestly sharing myself and opening up to them, in a way that is wise and compassionate to both of us?*

## PRACTICE 16
## Committing to the Most Beautiful Thing about You
## (Owl Intention #3)

"THE MOST BEAUTIFUL thing about a person you cannot see," a child wrote. What is the most beautiful thing about you? Do you have a sense of it? Do you dare to feel into it? Own it? Express it? Base your life upon it?

The most beautiful thing about ourselves may not be what we value most. How do we know what we value most? It's what we give most of our time and attention to. Our crocodile is ready to take up all of our attention, any time. In the Eastern wisdom traditions, they describe this as having a "Hungry Ghost" inside of us, a creature with a very big belly and a very small mouth, whose appetite is insatiable. Our crocodile is always hungry for more safety, more recognition, more followers, more money, more people who agree with me, more perfection, more control, more love, and more pleasure. Our current experience is never enough for the crocodile. And we aren't either. There is always something wrong with us that we need to fix. The crocodile sees growing as a self-improvement struggle to fill up an inner hole. The heart-based owl sees growth as a journey of remembering more and more who we truly are, the beauty inside of us, and bringing that to the foreground of our life and leadership.

So, what is that beauty inside of us? And how can we bring it more to the center of our lives? No one can tell us what's most beautiful about us—we get to discover this for ourselves. I sense it's something to do with the presence, the limitless sky of our being that we are in essence and how it expresses itself in endless ways that have love at their center.

See what happens when you allow yourself to spend some time with this most beautiful thing about you. It may give you direction about what your life is truly about, what you came here for. Having a sense of direction, a sense of purpose, helps guide us in our choices. Rooted in our purpose, we know clearly what to say yes to and what to say no to, like the river knows which way to flow around the rocks.

I think of Gene White, until recently President of the Global Child Nutrition Foundation. She has more energy than anyone I know, has dedicated her life to ending child hunger, and worked often sixteen-hour days until being in her mid-nineties. Gene has eyes that are so alive, always ready to learn something new. She treats everything in her life with purpose. Her husband passed a few years ago. Says Gene, "Isn't sadness just a way to adjust to what happened?" Even in the face of death, Gene stays centered in her unflinching commitment to life and discovery.

Inspired by others, like Gene, who live their most beautiful thing, we may become passionate to reclaim what we are truly about, and live and lead from that place. If we find that our most beautiful thing is about compassion, we treat each moment as such, also when people around us don't seem to be compassionate. If we sense we are about peace, we bring that intention to each moment, also when there is conflict. If we sense deep down we are about deep care, we extend that to others, without needing validation. Maybe we feel a great reservoir of creativity in us; then we can tap into that and bring that to the fore. It doesn't matter what we discover is our most beautiful thing. It's important that we recognize what it is and spend time and attention with it, being true to who we truly are, no matter what.

The crocodile may say, "Yes, but I don't know what my most beautiful thing is, so I can't commit to it either." That is understandable. Then we can remember that life is not about perfection, it's about progress. By our committing ourselves to be true to our most beautiful thing, our beauty opens, simply because we are spending time and attention on the question.

Our sense of our most beautiful thing may evolve over time. Maybe we begin by dedicating ourselves to something we already know is beautiful about us, like our curiosity, or firmness, or care, or simplicity, and apply that. As we practice this, we may discover other layers of beauty within us, like peace, unconditional love, and joy. Of course, these words cannot say what it is. That is for each of us to discover.

Being committed to this question, "What is the most beautiful thing about me?" in itself may become our center for a while. Sitting in traffic or having a cup of coffee in the morning, we keep an eye open for our inner beauty. Having a meeting, we stay committed to discovering more about our inner beauty. Launching a new project, we look at how we can bring our beauty to it. Given tough feedback, we do the same. Life provides endless opportunities for us to hold up a mirror to ourselves to discover what we are truly made of.

Once we have committed ourselves to this journey of discovering our beauty, we may tap into a sense of aliveness, even wonder. Then the discovery of our most beautiful thing in and of itself becomes the most beautiful thing.

## Leadership Practice

*See yourself through the eyes of a child. What is most beautiful about you? Spend some time with this question.*

*Then reflect on the following: What becomes possible for you when you spend more time and attention on your beauty and share that with others?*

# PRACTICE 17
## Leading from the Heart (Owl Intention #4)

O PEN YOUR EYES, your ears, your mouth, your hands, your heart.... Of all the ways we can open, the heart offers the deepest vistas into who we are. Opening our heart feels scary at times and also offers great relief. It requires courage, as we open ourselves to life, to others, and to ourselves, as we can't control what we open up to. The heart doesn't seem to discriminate.

Have you ever experienced pain? What happens when you close your heart to this experience? Chances are you felt more discomfort. Closing the heart is painful; it makes us rigid, anxious, and brittle. Contrast that with opening the heart, even to pain. A quiet strength comes online, a sense of warmth, connectedness, and care that envelops all thoughts, emotions, and sensations. With an open heart we find within ourselves a place to hold the pain—our own as well as that of others.

How do we lead with an open heart? And do we want to? Closed-hearted leaders will need to rely on their head and gut alone, missing out on a core part of their intelligence. Open-hearted leaders connect with a deeper source of wisdom and compassion in themselves. I find that when I allow my head's intelligence to be fueled by my heart's wisdom and compassion, I become a lot more adaptive, effective, and inspiring. From the head, I need to solve every problem logically, I see things as right and wrong and my experience becomes quite linear. Rooted in the heart, I become curious about the challenges on my path, dare to hold them lightly, take a walk with them, even play with them. I notice that instead of right and wrong, some things are more and others are less effective, relieving me from the heavy judgments manufactured by my head. And I start to see the broader connections between things, the nonlinearity of things, how what is happening over here impacts things over there, in ways that have not a one-to-one but a one-to-infinite relationship with each other.

From the heart, I live on the edge of discovery, always open, willing, and eager to learn new connections, to hold new paradoxes without forcing conclusions, to be with people and situations, comfortable or uncomfortable, without needing to react in a rush. Opening the heart a bit more, I connect more with the here and now. Opening the heart to my inner experience, I simply hold it, patiently care for it, without judgment. Insights come without my needing to force understanding. Experiences pass through my heart, without my being taken for a ride by them. Opening the heart to my outer experiences, I am not clinging to or cringing from them, I simply am with them and let the insight, the action—if anything at all—simply come up through the heart. Opening the heart, I find life a lot simpler, as I am anchored in a part of my being that exudes constancy, the constancy of the heart, that keeps beating, that keeps being with, that keeps opening, no matter what happens. The heart beats the drum of love.

This is not to say that I ignore the head. On the contrary. I plug my head's intelligence into the socket of heart power. Plugged in, I sense a wisdom, courage, and compassion arising in me that is far greater than my head can comprehend. Unplugged, the head's intelligence is weaker, more brittle, far more prone to worry and fear. Without the power that comes from the heart, my crocodiles tend to control my thinking mind—especially when I am under stress, which for the crocodiles is always.

Committed to staying plugged into my heart's power, I feel a sense of strength and confidence that is not dependent on outside circumstances or inside feelings. It's an energy inside of me that doesn't suffer when other parts of me are suffering. It's the energy in me that stays calm and in balance, when other parts of me want to run off after epic experiences, or run away from the painful ones. It's the energy in me that knows there is nothing I need to fear. It's the energy in me that knows that I am safe, no matter what happens.

Leading from the heart, we become a beacon of inspiration, safety, insight, compassion, and connectedness for ourselves and others. Leading from the heart, we find within ourselves the wherewithal to put ourselves in a place of service to what is needed now. Leading from the heart, we enjoy the beauty and wisdom of this moment.

---

## Leadership Practice

*Experiment with this. Close your heart for a moment. Close it even a bit more. What does it feel like? How does it impact your thinking?*

*Now open your heart, allow it to open. Now allow it to open a bit more and even a bit more. What do you experience now? What happens to your thoughts and feelings?*

*Repeat this two-part practice a few times during the day and notice what it's like to lead from the heart.*

# PRACTICE 18
## Giving (Owl Intention #5)

Y OU CAN ALWAYS, always give something, even if it's only kindness," wrote Anne Frank in her diary. It is a gift to give. On days where the self-absorbed mind is worried about this and that, the simple act of giving can restore us to a sense of flow, of connection with others and life. Giving provides us a sense of self-respect, of dignity.

Every moment we have a choice: Do we orient more to giving or getting? We have been so conditioned to always wanting more: get money, get a relationship, get approval, get a house, get a good feeling, get good grades, get it done, get stuff. The list of things we want to get seems to never end. And that makes sense, as our crocodilian fear-based mind keeps on fighting to validate our emotional sense of self. Getting money, a nice house, a partner, the next whatever, a great experience, are all ways for our crocodile to accrue a sense of self-worth, based on what we have. The crocodile tends to confuse *net worth* with *self-worth*. How much do I have in my bank account? How much pleasure did I get? How much did I get done? How much did I get people to like me? These are questions the crocodile keeps asking in its endless, yet fruitless search for a stable emotional identity. The more I have, the safer I will be, reasons the crocodile.

This is not to say that "getting" is bad. Of course, we need to get things, like a place to live, food, relationships, and experiences that nourish us. It's only that our crocodile over-indexes on getting, at the expense of everything else. The crocodile keeps consuming, even when we really don't need anything.

Given our crocodilian momentum oriented toward getting, it takes resolve to stay in a mindset of giving. How do we give at work? People often remember not what you did, but how you made them feel. That

60

gives us a clue of how we can give anywhere, anytime. We can always give our attitude. What attitude do you share with people? Do you share wisdom, compassion, kindness, firmness, empathy, understanding? Or does your crocodile unconsciously take over and have you share fear, judgment, blame, control, arrogance, and specialness? What energy do you give to each moment?

Being conscious of our own energy helps us be ready to gift it to others. I feel grateful for all the people I have worked with who shared with me an encouraging look, a kind word, or a way of speaking that made me feel, "Yes, I am welcome here." Our nonverbal cues can be such gifts to others. What would it be like if we entered our next conversation being slightly more purposeful about the energy we bring to it?

One crocodilian hallucination is that we have to feel good before we can do good. The crocodile believes this because it thinks that we are separate, disconnected from the source of life, presence, unconditional love. The opposite is true. We are always connected, it's just that we experience disconnection when we give in to our crocodilian self-talk and feeling states. I have noticed this when giving workshops. Some mornings, I don't feel well for whatever reason—maybe it's jet lag, or something at home I am concerned about, or a physical ailment, or whatever. My crocodile tells me to give up, to give in, and that I have nothing left to give. Well, if I give in to this self-talk, I guarantee myself the nothing-to-give-I-am-helpless-and-hopeless-experience. In moments like these, which are definitely uncomfortable, I have been learning to not do what my crocodile wants me to do and to instead do what my higher self wants me to do: to give my best, to be present to the people around me, and to serve them the best way I know how. Without fail, simply being grounded in the giving-intention provides the energy for giving and doing my work. It's not true that I have to feel great to give to others. Actually, if I don't feel great, it's a call for me to give more, not less. The more I give—including loving, not fear-coddling, attention to myself—the more I feel the energy of the bigger whole I am part of. Leading from the intention to give, I always have something to give, even if, as Anne Frank wrote, it is only kindness.

## *Leadership Practice*

*What does your crocodile want to get today? Check for yourself—Is it true that you really need this? Who would you be without this need for getting?*

*What can you give today? To whom? How can you give without any expectation to receive anything in return?*

# PRACTICE 19
## Clarity—Holding Perceptions Lightly (Owl Intention #6)

CLEAR SKY, CLEAR glasses, clear mind, clear thoughts—there is so much joy in having clarity, whether it's having clarity about where we want to go, a business dilemma, a relational issue, or anything else. With revelation comes a sense of relief.

My crocodile is not interested in real clarity at all. In a conversation, whether it's with myself or with another, my crocodile loves to muddy the waters, making big statements such as, "It's never going to work," "I feel overwhelmed," and "I think we are doing great." Staying at this level of abstraction, we tend to get lost in thoughts and feelings—our inner storyline. If we think, "I feel overwhelmed," and keep spinning at that level, soon we may think, "Because I feel overwhelmed, I am going to fail, and because I am going to fail, I should be scared, and because I am scared, I feel stressed, and because I feel stressed, I should rush, and because I rush, I start missing things, and because I start missing things, I fail," and so on. We can spend so much time in crocodilian melodrama, letting ourselves get sucked deeper and deeper into confusion, leading to more inaction, less effectiveness, and more stress and isolation.

We break out of this mental fog by turning on the light of inquiry. "What is really happening?" "What is a fact that underlies my thinking?" Pick one thought and one fact, not many; just pick one that you can look at in this moment, like an experiment that will help you draw conclusions about what really may be happening and where the real challenges may lie. Taking the example of "I am overwhelmed," we may find that underneath this thought lies the fact that we have three things to do and if we plan them well, we can get them done on time. Phew, another crocodilian fear thought bites the dust.

Insights don't always come when we want them to. Herein lies another element of seeing through the fog: patience. We need to have the patience to let the dust of our crocodilian projections settle. Our crocodile will keep us spinning, forcing us into answers, actions, and attitudes that are fear-based, only creating more confusion, adding more fog to the fog. Notice what happens when instead you breathe more deeply into your belly and let your crocodilian energy, which tends to show up in our shoulders and head, dissolve. When we relax, for example by breathing more deeply into the belly, we may notice another, quieter energy come online in us, something that may feel like presence, clarity, and peace.

With the patient eyes of presence, explore: What does your challenge look like? We can practice this by looking softly from our third eye center, the area between our eyebrows, while breathing consciously. Viewing a situation patiently, without rushing into crocodilian conclusions, we may start to see some patterns.

We may notice how our thought "I am overwhelmed" is only an interpretation we have put on top of our having three things to do today. As we patiently look at these thoughts, we go from "I *am* overwhelmed" to "I *have* overwhelming thoughts and feelings that I put on top of the reality of having three things to do." We have the overwhelm go from subject to object: we *are* no longer the overwhelm, we *have* overwhelming thoughts and feelings. We detach from this thinking and feeling by seeing that we have these thoughts rather than being identified with them. And we can detach even further by seeing that these are crocodile thoughts, for example, that I couldn't handle it, that I had to do it all today, and that there were too many things to do. From this awareness that we are not these crocodilian thoughts but rather just have them, more clarity arises.

For any crocodilian narratives that keep spinning despite our detaching from them, we can simply ask, "Is it true?" As we inquire more deeply we find out that no single thought we have is absolutely true, as all thoughts are only approximations of reality. A tree is not a tree, we simply call it a tree. A human being is not a human being, we simply call it that. Our thoughts are only pointers to reality.

No longer burdened by the illusion of having true thoughts, we start to see more clearly, with more lightness, into what may be going on. And we realize there is no such thing as perfect vision because our inner eyes aren't perfect. We only get glimpses of what is really going on. This doesn't preclude our wanting to find out. On the contrary, it magnetically attracts us to want to understand. Realizing our own imperfect vision, we are more and more drawn to the depth of our being, to see more clearly. We stay childlike in our curiosity and awe for what we don't know yet.

Holding our own perceptions lightly, we become more open and flexible to keep seeing the broader picture and letting insights emerge as they are ready, as gifts. Our greater openness leads to deeper wisdom. Deeper wisdom gives us the confidence to act decisively, boldly, knowing that we are coming from the deepest truth we have realized. We also know that our next action, coming from truth, will help to reveal more truth. For example, by speaking truthfully, we learn about truth. By listening deeply, we learn about depth. By acting generously, we learn about generosity. By acting from truth, we learn about the truth of our being.

Holding our perceptions lightly, we stay detached from holding on to any insight, realizing that every insight is only a stepping stone into another one in our endless journey of discovery. We hold our thoughts and actions lightly, rooted in presence, always in the intention to imbue our actions with as much depth as is available to us in this moment.

---

## Leadership Practice

*Reflect about a dilemma you are facing. What happens when you let go of any thoughts you have about it for a moment? Who are you without your thoughts about the dilemma? Then slowly, with a soft gaze in your mind, look into the dilemma again. What insights are emerging?*

## PRACTICE 20
### Simplicity Medicine (Owl Intention #7)

ONE CROCODILE MANY of us have involves our need to be special. Our crocodile doesn't want us to be just like everyone else. It wants us to be *the* generation, *the* best performer, *the* team, *the* company, *the* family, *the* country, the special one that stands out from the rest. We can spend so much of our time and attention on accruing specialness—through living in a special place, with special people, with special skills, with a special legacy...and the list goes on and on. If we give in to our hunger for specialness, we'll be forever running after more, because every time we reach some kind of epic height, we are already looking for our next one.

I have spent quite a bit of time and attention trying to satisfy this crocodile. I tried to get there by making lots of money; living in the center of the world, which I believed was New York City; trying to become famous; trying to become a great meditator, opera singer, teacher, and more. I even used being of service as a way to build my resume to become more special.

There is nothing wrong with having goals. However, looking back, I see how my quest for specialness was driven by my not feeling enough, trying to fill a deep hole of self-loathing and self-denial. I was too scared to be with myself as I was.

Slowly, I am learning to be with myself, just as I am, and to be with others, just as they are, without putting any expectations on any of us for how we should add to my special aura. I am discovering simplicity and the freedom that comes with that.

What is it like to be simple? One of the roots behind the word *simple* refers to a medicine made from one constituent, especially from one plant. I love that. I feel simplicity is a medicine itself. With an attitude of simply being with what is, comes self-acceptance. With self-acceptance comes self-love and with self-love comes love and acceptance for everyone and everything. Being simple, we don't need anything beyond our basic needs. Being simple, we can be at home, without any need for entertainment or distraction. We can simply enjoy this moment as it is. Being simple, we can be in a conversation, without an agenda of what should or shouldn't happen. We don't have to be the center of attention, nor do we need to hide in our very special corner.

Being simple, we take care of our finances. We make no special drama about not having enough or wanting more or having a lot. We simply live within our means. As a leader, with an attitude of simplicity, we don't try to be a great leader in the eyes of others. We simply lead by seeing what is needed and doing it. Seeing someone who is not performing well, we have a conversation with them, being able to stay with the facts, without a need to make it into a "thing." Working through a business challenge, we stay close to the facts and don't get ourselves entangled in all kinds of special-sounding business mumbo jumbo. We stay simple and do what is needed.

Being simple, we are more easily able to connect to our essence—a sense of unconditional love. We simply turn the other cheek of love to whatever is happening. There is such freedom in simply being. That is where simplicity leads me—simply being with what is, free from all the crocodilian stories about who I should be and what others should and should not be and do. I am simply here now.

Simplicity engenders quiet in me. The inner stillness that comes with simplicity becomes like a healing balm that encompasses everything. That stillness doesn't move, it simply is; whatever is happening, whether I have a lot or a little to do that day, whether people around me are happy or unhappy, whether we are making our goals or not, whether we are in the midst of an upswing or a downturn, my inner stillness simply is.

Simplicity may be one of the more powerful medicines we have that allows us to dispose of what we are not: a never-satisfied specialness-craving crocodilian hallucination that keeps wanting more. Dropping the cloak of specialness, we experience our inner lightness, the simplicity of being.

## Leadership Practice

*Make a list of the top five things you believe you need. Contemplate—Do I really need them? Who would I be without this need? What is left after I purge myself from the nonessentials?*


*Allow yourself to rest in the simple essence that lies beyond the nonessentials.*

# PART 3

## Facing Our Fears

# PRACTICE 21
## Working with Fear for Peace

PART OF US seems to always be bracing for something: Will I feel okay tomorrow? Will I be able to get my work done on time? How will they respond to my proposal? Will I stay healthy? Will I be strong enough? Our fearful crocodilian mind keeps feeding us fear thoughts. One of the roots of the word *fear* comes from the Dutch *gevaar*, which means "danger." Our crocodile believes we're always in some kind of danger and therefore we should brace ourselves for the worst.

Of course, there is nothing wrong with fear. It helps to protect us from dangerous situations, like an oncoming car in traffic, something about to fall on us, or aggression from other people. Unfortunately, our crocodilian mind, hell bent on our egoic survival, doesn't know how to work wisely with fear. Instead of using fear as an input, working with it, questioning it, and responding to it wisely, it reacts to it immediately, even identifying with the fear. We mistake the cloud (the fear) in the sky of our awareness for the sky itself. We lose perspective, and soon all we can see is our fearful projection of reality. Fearful of not getting our work done, we start feeling overwhelmed and react by giving in to anxiety and overwork. Fearful of someone leaving us, we obsess over what we have done wrong, why they are to blame, and what we should do to fix it now. Afraid someone is not going to like our proposal, we don't say anything at all, feeling resentful for not having spoken our truth, bottling up our feelings. Or we overwork, over-explain, and try to manipulate the other into liking our work.

What if we related differently to our fears? What if we saw fear as just another input from our nervous system? As a captain on a ship, we can simply look at the fear dispassionately, and inquire into it. Is it true that I should fear this? Is it absolutely true? Who do I become when I give in to this fear? And how would I respond differently if I no longer gave in to this fearful reactivity?

We can start our inquiry into our fear by noticing it in our energy. Fearful thinking tends to have a quality of panic, anxiety, and rush to it. It wants us to react *now*, or else...! Alternatively, it can also produce a state of numbness, inertia, and paralysis. Working wisely with our fear, we can press our internal pause button, take a few deep breaths, and ask a few questions: Is this fear true? What parts of my egoic identity—for example, "I am good," "I am competent," "I am nice," or "I am special"—is this fear trying to protect? What would happen if I dropped these ego protection strategies? Then what becomes possible for me?

Fear is like a petulant child. It tends to not give up easily. It will assert, reassert, and come back at us in many forms, sometimes screaming for our attention. The fearful part of our mind starts its development in our earliest years. It bases its danger assessment on stories we learned when we got here and as we grew up as children. In our early years, the mind learns very quickly what is dangerous and what is safe—don't get too close to the hot stove, otherwise you'll burn yourself; when you lock your door you'll be ok; don't eat something toxic. That is the good news. The bad news is that the mind's bookkeeping of what is safe and what is not is imprecise. It stores an experience of an unsatisfied parent as "my world is coming to an end and I have to fix this now," a low grade in school as "I am a failure," and classmates who mock me as "I am ridiculous." Over the years, we stuff ourselves with fear-based drama that occupies more and more of our mind space. As a consequence, we start to see less and less clearly, more and more from our fearful projections, and less and less from truth.

That's why asking ourselves the simple question, "Is this true?" is so healing. The contemplation of what is true restores us to sanity. It restores us to seeing reality as it is, not as our crocodilian mind has us believe it to be. However, as with any good movie, our crocodilian mind is very convincing, producing a compelling fearful undercurrent in us. Under the influence of the horror movie of our crocodilian hallucinations, of what we believed to be reality for a few hours, days, months, or even years, it may take a while to shake these anxious feelings. Did you ever feel scared after having watched a horror movie?

Working with our fearful mind requires gentle patience and firm resolve. Sure, we may feel anxious for a while longer, even after we have taken a few deep breaths and have questioned our fearful thinking. In these moments, we can remind ourselves that feelings are not facts. In fact, they are often only echoes of the crocodile's horror movies we have been watching. We can also practice a slogan I learned recently: *Don't do what you want to do and do what you don't want to do.* In other words, don't follow the instructions of your fearful crocodilian mind. Instead, act on the wise counsel from your owl, even if the anxiety in your body hasn't quite caught on yet that your FEAR was only "False Evidence Appearing Real."

## Leadership Practice

*Notice any fearful thought you have right now. What would it have you believe about what is true? Who would you be without this belief? How can you respond to the moment in front of you from a wiser, more compassionate place?*

# PRACTICE 22
## Standing on the Shoulders of Our Seven Fear Families

W̶E DON'T GET to stay in our mother's womb, our warm bed, our comfy job, or our predictable relationship patterns. As we engage with life, it continues to invite us to grow, to shed old ways of being and behaving and to adopt new ones. Part of us loves growth. Another part would prefer to keep everything the same as we know it. We tend to love and fear growth. Will I still be able to provide for my family if I pursue more of my authentic purpose more fully? Will my relationships survive my authenticity? Will I still be successful if I focus on what I really want to do?

Our crocodile keeps feeding us fearful narratives to keep us from growing. The crocodile wants us to doubt ourselves so we stay safe. One way to free ourselves from our fearful self-talk is to recognize it and the patterns it comes in. Fear comes in different flavors, related to different motivations we have in life.

With our motivation to be financially secure comes a fear of not having enough. With our interest to be in relationships, we meet our fear of being abandoned. With our desire to make something of ourselves comes the fear of failure. And when we develop an interest to learn about ourselves, we get to face the fear of uncertainty. Each of our motivations also births fear. When we want to make a difference in the lives of others, we may hesitate to follow through, afraid we might get hurt as people may not receive us well, or concerned that we may hurt them with our assertiveness. The more we open to life, the more we may develop the yearning to understand it. In our quest for understanding, we may come face to face with our fear of complexity and overwhelm. And as we become keener to understand who we truly are and our place in the universe, our sense of identity may get challenged and we may experience the fear of losing everything we know, including knowing who *we* are.

In our lives we meet these fears over and over again. You may notice a correlation between these fears and Maslow's hierarchy of needs. To make them easier to recognize, I have organized them into seven fear categories, each relating to a different universal human motivation. We tend to learn these fears through our life experiences and much of it gets handed down through the communities we grew up in. That's one reason we also call these seven fear categories seven Fear *Families*—we inherit them from the people we grew up with and they inherited them from their communities. Take a look at the table below and see which of these seven Fear Families has the most power in your life right now:

|   | Motivation | Fear Family |
|---|---|---|
| 1 | Survival | Scarcity |
| 2 | Relationship | Abandonment |
| 3 | Self-esteem | Failure |
| 4 | Discovery | Uncertainty |
| 5 | Making a difference | Hurt |
| 6 | Cohesion | Complexity |
| 7 | Wisdom and compassion | Losing identity |

How does the Fear Family that is most dominant in your life want you to act out? What reactive patterns are you falling into under the influence of this Fear Family? For example, if you fear not having enough, you may over-index your self-talk by worrying about your future, overworking, looking for quick fixes, or possibly giving up and taking a victim-stance, blaming others. If you are driven by the fear of abandonment, you may spend a lot of time pleasing others or judging people who don't fit with your clique, as a way to stay with the tribe. If the fear of failure is active in you, you may either play it safe or try to micromanage and perfect yourself and others. If you are afraid of the unknown, you may run toward what you know or rigidly hold on to what you think you know, including beliefs and behaviors that are limiting your effectiveness. Afraid of hurt, you may stifle your own expression by not saying what you really have to say, or spend time being resentful that others don't intuitively get what you are all about. Overcome by the fear of complexity, you may rush to conclusions or masquerade as the one who knows. And driven by the fear of losing your sense of who you are, you may invest energy in building a special identity—being "better than"—and demanding people's time and attention for you.

There is nothing wrong with any of these fears or how our crocodile tries to compensate for them by having us resort to coping behaviors. It's part of the curriculum of life. Take a moment and just accept whatever Fear Family is active in you and all the hard work your crocodile is doing to help you to stay safe. Thank your crocodile, the inner child in you who is scared—and has been most, if not all, of your life.

Then ask yourself: Who would I be without this fear? Without the fear of scarcity—not worrying as much about not having enough—how much time and attention could I free up to spend on doing what I really need to do? Without the fear of abandonment, what opportunities do I see to build truly authentic and empathetic relationships? Dropping the fear of failure, how much more effectively can I live my purpose, no longer distracted and intimidated by little or bigger bumps in the road? Letting go of the fear of uncertainty, how much more of an adventure life becomes to joyfully discover more every day? No longer impeded by the fear of pain and hurt, how much stronger a contribution can I make to others? What if I loved complexity; then how much more learning could I do, letting insights come naturally to me as the dust of my mind's feverish machinations settles? And how much freedom, love, and peace would I experience, no longer as concerned about who I am as a separate person?

We can choose to stand on the shoulders of our Fear Families. Each Fear Family is a portal for us to let go a part of us that is not true and no longer serves us. As we do so, we discover greater resilience, connectedness, and possibilities to truly take care of what is needed now.

## Leadership Practice

*Which of the seven Fear Families is most active in you? Take a moment to thank it for all the hard work this crocodile has been doing to help you stay safe.*

*Now imagine yourself letting go a bit more of this Fear Family. How would you feel? How would you relate to others? How will you lead differently?*

## PRACTICE 23
## Plenty of Love to Go Around
## Taming the Scarcity Crocodile

D O YOU SOMETIMES worry that you may not have enough to eat, pay your bills, keep your home, or maintain your standard of living? Worry has a quality of paralysis and excess built into it. Completely obsessed by worry, we lose our sanity. Overcome by fear, we no longer act and think rationally. We see everything as black and white, win-lose, I am going to make it or I am not.

The first of our Fear Families is the fear of scarcity. It's a very old fear and a basic one that drives many of our worries in some way. It sends us into an irrational downward spiral of negative thinking. And it can be very convincing—our very survival is at stake!

Something happens in our nervous system when we confuse *care for* with *worry about*. There is nothing insane about caring to make sure we have food on the table, a place to live, and good education for our children. However, our fearful crocodilian mind exaggerates, making up stories that have us believe that everything poses a disastrous threat to us.

Under the influence of the fear of not having enough, we worry. We tell ourselves we need to work and never rest, always rushing to the next thing. We tell ourselves others' success is our loss. We believe that we will never have enough, that to reach the elusive goal of safety we need to accumulate, accumulate, accumulate. When things don't go our way, we become aggressive and blame others, making others wrong and ourselves right. We believe our sense of being right will make us stronger in our never-ending battle for survival. We believe that making others wrong will weaken them, giving us an advantage. We over-prepare and try to anticipate all scenarios.

Paradoxically, our crocodilian fear of scarcity chews up tons of resources—our own time and attention and that of others. The more we are focused on scarcity, the less resourceful we become to address our real needs. We can remember the cost of this fear as follows:

*My Actual Resourcefulness* = *My Full Potential Resourcefulness—* *(My Fear of Scarcity + My Other Fears)*

I see the fear of scarcity play out when I wake up. Driven by this fear, which for me often manifests in thinking I don't have enough time, I feel anxious. If I give in to this anxiety, I may skip my morning meditation and writing practices and jump right into my email, trying to get as much done as possible. By giving in to my scarcity crocodile, I cut myself off from the energy-giving flow of life, which I in part access through spending time and attention on the source of my resourcefulness, the ground of my being—presence, unlimited potential.

I have a choice. I don't need to give in to the crocodilian fear-mongering of my mind. I can choose again. I can choose to let go of this fearful thinking, rather than giving in to it. This requires an inner resolve, as the crocodilian anxious momentum can be fierce. In these moments where my crocodile tries to overwhelm me with fear, I simply tell myself: I love myself and I have enough. I love myself and I have enough.

Ask yourself: On a scale from 1 to 10 how much do you love yourself? What would happen if you loved yourself at 10? What would it feel like?

Yes, I know, loving yourself seems like a strange antidote to scarcity. Try it out anyway. Say to yourself: *I love myself.* Loving myself, I may discover a sense of ease, a sense of flow that rinses out all worried thoughts. Loving myself, I access inner clarity and strength. Loving myself, I see my fearful crocodile for what it is: a passing cloud on the screen of my awareness. It's only a pocket of energy. I am not that passing cloud. Loving myself, I can learn to love that energy and let it go. I can simply hug it briefly as I would hug a child, without having to change my day for it or let it distract me from what I need to focus on.

Loving myself, I focus on what matters. Focusing on what matters helps me to take care of what is needed now. Loving myself may be the best investment I can make to ensure I bring my best self to every moment. With my best self, I access an inner resourcefulness that somehow knows how to address the challenges that come on my path—including those that are about my basic survival needs.

---

## Leadership Practice

*Consider how the fear of scarcity shows up in your day. How do you react under the influence of the fear of scarcity?*

*Practice loving yourself at 10. Notice how it changes the energy you bring to any challenge you may face today. How can you respond to the challenge differently, grounded in greater self-love?*

# PRACTICE 24
## Daring to Be Genuine
## Taming the Abandonment Crocodile

"I WON'T BE ABLE to be truthful with them," "They just don't get it," "I should play nice with them," and "I'm better off just doing it myself," says our crocodile, thinking about others. Relating to others brings both the best and the worst in us to the surface. Giving appreciation, deeply understanding someone or being understood, touching someone deeply or being touched, discovering things together, feeling loved and loving—sharing can be so life-affirming. Great relationships help us feel taller, more whole on the inside, and more connected with everyone, not just the person we are relating with.

We also experience many of our deepest hurts in relationships—feeling judged, shamed, ridiculed, excluded, controlled, suffocated, and held back are some of the many ways relationships can be challenging. Most of us want to relate. In fact, we have to relate if we want to survive. We are deeply dependent on each other. Even if we live by ourselves, we are still dependent on others for our food, shelter, and health. This is really bad news for our crocodile; it's always afraid that we will lose the relationships we depend on and die. A core fear in our crocodilian system is the fear of abandonment.

As with all fears, our crocodile exaggerates and doesn't see things from our true perspective. Our crocodile sees everything from the perspective of a separate me, our ego, that needs constant protection and validation. Looking for protection, our crocodile tells us to hold back, and to not tell the truth. It says, "Others won't be able to handle your truth. They will leave you." Are you able to handle the truth of people that can't handle your truth leaving you? Being ourselves in relationships is an act of bravery. Being genuine requires us to be confident enough in ourselves that we are okay no matter how people around us respond. Being in a relationship with others requires us to first be able and willing to be in a relationship with ourselves.

The word *genuine* has the Latin word *genu* in it, which means "knee." It refers to the Roman custom of a father acknowledging paternity by placing the child on his knee. Being genuine asks us to be willing to embrace our truth and be willing to hold it, like a child, taking full responsibility for it. Are we willing to be that brave and be with our truth, completely?

Being genuine is an act of caring, starting with ourselves. We need to be willing to hold ourselves, our true selves, and the deepest truth we have realized, with care. As we hold our truth with care, we may feel compelled to share our truth with others, also with care. We want to share what we see, without imposing it on others, while remaining gentle and kind with the truth that comes from within us.

Our crocodile can't handle our truth and wants to put it away, afraid of what others may say, or, conversely, parades it around as a way to confirm its specialness. And our crocodile has no patience for or interest in other people's truth. It sees other people's truth as threatening, or less than, or more than, always comparing. Our crocodile's first reaction to anyone else is "How will they hurt or help me?" Our crocodile doesn't see people in and of themselves. Our crocodile sees people as part of its own survival strategies. Our crocodile judges, shames, complies, pleases, manipulates, or whatever other strategy it deems necessary for its own emotional survival.

Controlled by the fear of abandonment, we abandon ourselves and our truth and also abandon others and their truth. Living out the fear of abandonment is a painful experience—thankfully so; as our nervous system tells us by experiencing the pain of rejection and disconnect, it's time to reflect and see another way. The pain of rejection is a call for love—to be with, as opposed to run away from, our own truth and that of others.

Who would you be without the fear of abandonment? Maybe this is too far of a stretch for you. Hold both the fear and the truth about yourself with love. See what happens when you allow yourself to become truly present to both aspects of yourself.

You may experience an inner quiet, even warmth. You may find that your reactivity and compulsion to stuff your truth, or judge or please others, becomes less urgent. You may recognize in yourself the little tender child who knows your deeper truths. And you may find respect for others, even care, for their truth, and also empathy for their fearful child—who, just like you, is afraid of being abandoned.

What would happen if you committed to no longer abandoning anyone? This doesn't mean you put yourself in hurtful situations. You can even choose to be with people from a distance, in silence, extending the presence that you are, the love that you are, without words.

See what becomes possible for you when you fully commit to being with yourself and others, no matter what.

## Leadership Practice

*Reflect on a challenging relationship you have. What is really true for you about this relationship? What fears do you have? Who would you be without these fears?*

*Take a moment and watch both your truth and your fear sitting side by side within you. Now hold the other person in mind and hold their fear and truth with equal care. What do you experience?*

*How can you relate to yourself and the other more from your true self?*

## PRACTICE 25
### From Perfect Little Me to Purposefulness
### Taming the Failure Crocodile

FAILURE IS NOT the end of the road. It's only one step on the endless road we are traveling. Of the seven Fear Families, fear of scarcity, abandonment, failure, uncertainty, hurt, complexity, and losing identity, the fear of failure is for many of us the most energy-consuming. In our fear polls, people say that fear of failure is one of their top fears, and understandably so.

When did you get a good grade in school? Was it because you asked a good question or made a mistake, or because you gave the right answer? And what did your caregivers say to you when you were able to say your name right for the first time? We have been conditioned to get it right. We didn't grow up appreciating failure. We grew up trying to avoid it, for some of us at all cost. I remember in school checking my exam paper about five times before I turned it in. I was dead set on getting a perfect grade. Anything else would feel like utter defeat to me. I still see this today. I want my home to be perfect at all times, food needs to be prepared just so, even my body has to be a certain way. Or at least this is what my crocodile keeps telling me. Do it perfectly or don't bother at all.

Driven by the fear of failure, I try to micromanage everything: when my assistant schedules my appointments, how my clients respond to what I say, what my partner says and doesn't say, even writing this book. I need to write every page perfectly. My fear-of-failure crocodile turns life into a stressful win-lose tournament that never ends. This crocodile stresses me out and has me treat others as tools to keep building my perfect little world.

What is failure really? The word *failure* comes from Anglo-Norman French *failer*, which means "nonoccurrence" and "cessation of supply."

When we fail, it simply means that something other than what we expected is occurring, which our crocodile judges as a problem. Did you ever receive negative feedback that you couldn't stop thinking about the rest of the day? Chances are your fear-of-failure crocodile was obsessing about why something turned out differently than expected, blaming yourself and others. You see, the crocodile has us live in a very narrow band of what reality is acceptable and safe to us and what is not. Anything that falls outside of that narrow band the crocodile deems as bad. It hopes that by obsessing somehow we will be able to regain control and put reality back in line with our expectations.

We can also approach failure differently. We can see it as *"different-than-expected reality."* What we had in mind didn't occur. What does failure feel like when we drop our expectations about what should happen? Then failure simply becomes something that happens without our having to take it personally. Yes, we may learn from it, but we are not wasting energy trying to bend reality back to our will by denying what happened, by obsessing over it, or by furiously trying to force a quick-fix solution.

The Cherokee people say, "Listen to the whispers so you don't have to hear the screams." What if our failures were simply cracks in our self-construed sense of reality? What if failures were the whispers that can help us see ourselves and our situation with fresh eyes? What if our failures are actually doorways to free us from old beliefs we held, that we were superimposing on reality, believing that they would keep us safe?

When my home is not perfectly in order, I can see it as a failure I should worry about. Or I can see it as a doorway to greater freedom. I ask myself, "Is it true that my home should be in perfect order?" Of course not. Even asking the question gives me some relief, and ironically restores some sense of order in myself, where I had started to feel mental chaos. My home having some chaos turns into an opportunity for me to let go of a belief in perfection that I thought would keep me safe. Perfectionism is actually a prison I put myself and others in, rather than the safe haven I had imagined it to be.

Focused on never failing, I lose sight of the bigger picture. Focusing on one so-called misstep, I lose sight of the road that I am traveling on. Alternatively, I can use the discomfort of a so-called misstep to focus my attention and bring me back to reality, and to the destination I am walking toward. As opposed to giving in to the fear of failure, I can focus on my purpose. I can use every failure as a moment of letting go of the false expectations I had and connecting more deeply to what I really care about, which goes much beyond my having my perfect little crocodilian experience.

---

## Leadership Practice

*Think of a failure you had recently. How is it a teacher to help you let go of your expectations—for example, of perfection?*

*What is the bigger purpose you are committed to? What happens when you refocus your time and attention on that, rather than obsessing about what may not have gone according to your plan?*

# PRACTICE 26
## The Heart of Discovery
### Taming the Uncertainty Crocodile

WHAT WILL HAPPEN tomorrow? Will I have enough money? Will they like my proposal? Will I be able to do my work? Will I be healthy? Our fearful crocodile keeps whispering worry thoughts about our uncertain future. Ponder for a moment how the word *uncertainty* feels to you. Is it exciting? Or maybe it has an element of worry associated with it?

In the dictionary the word *uncertainty* is explained as "the quality or state of being uncertain—doubt." Who wants that?!? Who needs doubt? Our survival-oriented crocodile definitely doesn't. Uncertainty equals the possibility of danger, says the crocodile. And we need to get rid of danger as quickly as possible. The crocodile rushes in, trying to fix our sense of uncertainty by having us worry, become rigid, close our mind off to what is true and possible—in some cases it even puts up a wall between us and reality by creating drama. If I create drama, thinks the crocodile, at least I am in charge. The more drama I create—by complaining, playing the martyr, or creating conflict—the greater the sense of certainty I have. Drama is one of the favorite go-tos of my crocodile. It feels familiar to me—I know what it's like to feel sad and helpless, or angry and judgmental. These are familiar spots for my crocodile to hang out. Cuddled in the bosom of drama, I don't need to face the uncertainty of reality, which the crocodile projects to be bad. Why? Better safe than sorry, thinks the crocodile. My job is to help you stay safe, and so it's better for you to over-index on danger rather than to underestimate potential threats. You only die once, believes the crocodile.

Giving in to this fearful crocodile, I lose touch with what's actually happening. I am not seeing what's really happening, as I am obsessed by my crocodilian projections. I don't see reality, and I become ineffective, and often hurtful to others. Aren't others one of the greatest sources of uncertainty, and therefore danger to me? reasons my crocodile. With my head rigid and my heart closed, I judge, manipulate, make wrong, obsess over, and become a victim to others—all sure ways to undermine my relationships. Paradoxically, giving in to the fear of uncertainty, I create a very unstable world for myself, with broken relationships, ineffective behaviors, and tons and tons of self-doubt and blame.

What would it be like to see uncertainty with different eyes, possibly the eyes of the heart? How would we see uncertainty then? Maybe as something we can be curious about, possibly even enjoy, as the great unfolding adventure of life and leadership we get to participate in for the few short years we are on this planet. Our head will keep saying "yes but" and "what if." Our heart has no need to understand and reason. It simply opens, like a mother opens her arms to her child, without any agenda—being there for life, with all its ups and downs and sideways happenings.

Grounded in our heart, we discover a sense of unrelenting strength, possibly even courage. Courage has the Latin word *cor* in it, which means "heart." With an open heart we access our courage, which we can bring to any situation we face. Conversely, when we greet the uncertainty of the day with a closed heart, it becomes a to-do list that we need to complete as quickly and as safely as possible. We glom on to pseudo-certainties, like our inbox, our text messages, our checking account, or instant-gratification fast food. Come to think of it, we have created a society that tries to outflank the uncertainty of life. We do our utmost to get rid of uncertainty. Our phone tells us what the weather will be tomorrow, how many minutes it will take for the Uber to get us where we're going, what the stock market will be doing, where our friends and families are, what we should watch today, even what we should eat or think now. We are being stuffed with information that tries to protect us from experiencing one of the fundamental truths of life: It's always changing and it's uncertain.

Of course, there is nothing wrong with any of this technology, as long as we don't use it as a crocodilian crutch where we navigate life with our phones rather than our hearts. We can use our phone as an instrument in the service of what our heart tells us, and the same goes for the thinking in our head. We can make our head a support to help us live and lead from our heart's wisdom.

Committed to living from the heart, uncertainty simply becomes an invitation for us to open our heart a bit more. As opposed to closing our heart, when new information or another new trigger hits us, we open our heart a bit further. We use our everyday uncertainties as ways to stretch our hearts open. Committed to living from the heart, we drop all our sense of "I am right, and I know." Committed to living from the heart, uncertainty turns into fuel for our ongoing journey of discovery, about what this life is and who we are in it. With an open heart, life becomes an adventure we get to play a part in.

## Leadership Practice

*Consider something you feel has a great deal of uncertainty in it. How does your crocodile want you to react to it? In what ways may it try to create pseudo-certainty by holding on to familiar beliefs, feelings, and behavioral patterns?*

*What happens when you commit to open your heart to this uncertain aspect of your life and leadership a bit more? What happens with the wisdom, compassion, and peace that is available to you? How can you share this energy with others?*

## PRACTICE 27
## From Smokescreen into the Fire of Truth
## Taming the Hurt Crocodile

Yes, no, maybe. Do you dare to speak with clarity? I remember a time when I felt spasms in my throat when the topic of homosexuality was being discussed at the dinner table. I felt intense shame about having feelings for other men and didn't feel safe to say anything about it. Come to think of it, I have a PhD in withholding what I really think and feel. When my partner asks me how I feel, my pat response will be, "Oh, I am great," even when I am not. Fortunately, he doesn't buy into my smokescreen talk. He will respond, "Hmm mmm..." looking me directly in the face, as if to say, "Tell me how you really are."

My crocodiles don't want me to be clear and honest. They would rather have me hold back and play it safe, as opposed to taking my chances. My crocodile doesn't like authentic expression, just like our consensus consciousness, the way we have been socially conditioned, has taught us to shy away from sharing our selves openly. The first definition in the dictionary of the word *vulnerable* is "capable of being physically or emotionally wounded"; the second: "open to attack or damage." We are conditioned to perceive vulnerability as a problem rather than a strength.

Inauthenticity is costly and cunning. It shows up in our not saying what we really mean. We make inauthentic choices, suffocating ourselves trying to comply with the expectations we believe others have of us. I didn't "come out" until my late twenties—or even allow myself to have an intimate experience with another man until then. My crocodiles had expertly woven a thick screen around this part of myself—that had also become impenetrable to myself. I wasn't even sure any more what my preferences were. When a lovely woman asked me on a date, I was so relieved. At least I didn't have to deal with my own homophobia any more—or so I thought.

Fortunately, life had other plans for me. Life can be fierce in its challenge to our smokescreens. I fell deeply in love with a man I had known well. At some point, there was no denying it anymore. Every fiber in my being said, "Yes, Hylke, you need to do this. You need to open yourself to being with another man." This newfound intimacy was the most natural thing. I had imagined I was going to be averse to touching another body that looked like mine, like I wouldn't know what to do. And the opposite was true. Being with him was as natural to me as taking a walk and as fulfilling as the beautiful music I had played as a child.

Stepping through the fear of hurt, we discover how life-giving being truly authentic can be—not only for ourselves, but also for the people around us. When we give ourselves the permission to be authentic, it gives other people the permission to do the same. I see this in workshops. Often, I ask the leader of the group to do a fishbowl with me at the beginning of the session. A fishbowl is a conversation between a few people in front of the group, where we simulate being in someone's living room and having a deeply honest conversation, forgetting for a moment that other people are listening in. The more honest the leader is about what they really care about, what their fears and insecurities are, and what they want for the group, the more honest the conversations the rest of the day become. Honesty is a lighthouse that helps others find their way home to their authenticity.

Not being honest with ourselves leads us to living borrowed lives. We listen to other people's expectations rather than our own inner compass. It's a whole lot safer, says our crocodile, to fit with the tribe, who is petrified of anyone disagreeing with them. Giving in to these crocodiles chews up lots of our time and attention. Soon we have little energy left to dedicate to our lives, to give ourselves to our true gifts, to what we are here to contribute. As opposed to pursuing our dreams, we throw our lives away pursuing other people's dreams—for example, the dreams of some corporations who wish to keep us in a shopping and entertainment frenzy, 24/7. Spending time to listen to what we really want, what is truly fulfilling to us, takes courage. Yes, we may find ourselves alone for a while. Some people who we thought were friends may fade away. And we may have to become honest with ourselves about ways in which we are not living authentically, even how we may be addicted to some of these forms of inauthentic, crocodilian living.

As leaders, we may need to stand up to our colleagues and teams when we find that we are not in alignment with our deepest values. No longer deterred by the fear of being hurt, or of hurting others, we say what we need to say, standing for ourselves, while not standing against anyone.

Beware: The crocodile knows how to bend anything to its will, even authentic expression. Driven by the fear of hurt, we may try to dominate others, shut them out, or try to rescue them, thinking we're expressing our highest values. We can check ourselves by asking: Why Am I Talking?— or, in short, WAIT. Am I talking to satisfy a crocodilian need to be safe and seen as important, even essential, trying to live up to some sort of identity I try to hold on to? Or am I truly coming from the ground of my being, presence, unconditional love, that doesn't need anything and is only here to give, to extend its essence?

## Leadership Practice

*On a scale from 1 to 10, how much am I in touch with my true gifts? What are they? How can I express them even more?*

*How would my crocodile want me to build a sense of identity around these gifts? How could I be truly authentic without the need of having to be someone?*

## PRACTICE 28
### The Silence Underneath the Chaos
### Taming the Complexity Crocodile

How MUCH ARE you at home in dilemma, paradox, contradiction, and chaos? Our crocodile likes things nice and neat, so it knows what it can count on for its survival. Our crocodile will force clarity even if there is none to be had yet. It will force a group to come to conclusions before it's time. It will panic without a clear answer. "Oh, we'll see" is about as terrifying to this crocodile afraid of complexity as jumping off a cliff.

We're wired for clarity. We find such relief in finding out what happens at the end of a movie. At the same time, we're drawn to the mystery of existence, never quite knowing what we will learn today.

Resting in our essence, presence, unconditional love, we may experience a sense of clarity that is ongoing, especially when we rest our attention between our eyebrows, at our third eye. This is not clarity we make happen, it's clarity that happens to us. It is clarity that comes as a gift. We experience this clarity, like we experience a clear blue sky. We become clear on the inside. This can be a very peaceful experience—completely clear about who we are and what is true. And even from that clear place, we still experience unanswered questions. The difference is that *we* are clear while experiencing complexity. We don't lose our sense of clarity while in the midst of complexity.

For the crocodile this is impossible. For the crocodile *everything is about me*, so complexity and lack of clarity means there is something that we need to figure out now, for us to be safe; or alternatively, overwhelmed by the complexity, we check out, another way for the crocodile to simulate a sense of clarity. If we try to solve everything now, we tend to resort to the answers we know, thinking we should be the sapient one who knows. Also, being a doomsday prophet can be a good strategy to solve for complexity, thinks the crocodile. *This is just too complex, so the world is going to end...and at least I know, so I don't have to engage any more with the mucky muck of existence.* Or we check out altogether, hiding out in our little fantasy la-la land bubble as if the complexity is none of our concern. Being sapient, doomsday, or in la-la land, we disconnect from what is happening—and from others around us and from our true selves, unlimited presence, that knows none of the artificial boundaries our crocodilian mini-mind imposes on reality.

We become self-absorbed rather than self-giving. This doesn't feel good—fortunately, as life tries to help us break out of our box by giving us discomfort. Waking up to the realization that we were driven by a crocodilian mini-mind hallucination, we may choose to not stay in the hallucination, but rather step out of it, opening ourselves to the full catastrophe of pain, paradox, and chaos that is part of life and leadership.

When we rest as presence, this is ok. We don't need anything to be clearer than it is now. *We simply stay present to what is, ready to receive any insights that may come from within us, or from what other people and situations around us are teaching us.* I remember sitting on a conference call to decide on the *from-tos* in mindset and behaviors that were going to be the focal point of a two-year culture journey for a group of about two thousand people. I had done my homework and studied all the opinions we had gathered through speaking with dozens of people in the organization. I had written down my five from-to statements, and my crocodile was ready for the group to adapt them. I remember my crocodile even thinking, "Maybe we don't even need to have this meeting, as I have it all figured out already."

Not so fast, said life. I shared my findings and other team members shared theirs. Together we debated for about two hours and together we discovered a much richer picture of what was important for us to focus our culture work on than my wanting-the-answer-now-crocodile had anticipated. I have heard it described as daring to stay in the "groan zone" in a conversation. Yes, it may be uncomfortable to the crocodile, who wants to force clarity now and who may want to be seen as the Sapient One who knows and came up with the answer. Yet waiting for the dust to settle may be one of the most helpful contributions we can make in our journey toward clarity.

## Leadership Practice

*Once you've used a meditation tool to quiet your mind a bit, consider this:*

*Think of a problem that is important to you where you don't have an answer yet. How do you feel about this? What conclusions has your crocodile drawn about your not having the answer yet (e.g., I am ... [incompetent, weak, stupid, irresponsible, lazy...])?*

*Who would you be without these confusions about yourself? What happens when you allow yourself to get really still and sit with the complexity, without your having to solve for it? Then what do you discover? What is becoming clear to you?*

# PRACTICE 29
## Let "You" Be Temporary—Taming the Identity Crocodile

L OOK AT ME, says our crocodile. Look at how special I am, how much I have, what I contribute, how much people love me, and how I am better than. Or conversely, look at how difficult my life is, how I can never do enough, how much people don't appreciate me, and how I am less than. The crocodile keeps fantasizing a string of images about who we are, afraid of the great nothingness that we may fall into—a complete death of our identities, you might say—if we let go of who we think we are.

We are taught to be better than or worse than from an early age. In school we get a higher or lower grade than the person sitting next to us; if our GPA and resume are strong enough we may get that scholarship; and even in the mating game we are taught that we need to be more beautiful, kinder, and more emotionally skillful to be able to land and hold on to a mate. In our consensus-consciousness reality, we keep convincing ourselves that how we stack up to others really matters to who we are. How many followers did you get? How epic was your vacation? Or, conversely: How traumatic has your life been? How hard was your day?

The crocodile keeps a measuring stick at hand at all times. We are in constant competition with our self-imposed standards of better or worse than, never quite feeling good enough. I am grateful that we don't find peace in our pursuit of the perfect self-image. Unrest is a great motivator to keep looking for a more truthful perspective on life and leadership. Without unrest, we might be lulled into believing that our perspective is true.

Who would we be without any and all of our identities, like I am special, better than, nicer than, worse than, a martyr, a hero, a nothing, the Savior, the One Who Knows it All, the Ignoramous, a victim, or a perpetrator?

We're not saying here that identities aren't helpful. For example, it helps to take on the identity of a caregiver, a manager, a listener, etc., as the situation calls for it. However, the crocodile doesn't use our identities to be of service to life; it grabs them to construct and curate an ever more sophisticated fortress of beliefs about who we are. Our fearful crocodile confuses our temporary identities with the eternal and wants us to invest all our energies into spinning a more and more convincing story about who we are. It believes we can somehow out-fantasize the reality of our true being.

Deep, deep down, we all know that any story we tell ourselves is just a story. These stories can be helpful to orient us, to motivate us, to calm us, to comfort us. However, they can never take the place of reality. There is no story that can tell us who we truly are. Who would we be without our story about ourselves?

Take a few deep breaths into the belly, then continue reading. Who would we be without our beliefs about who we are? At first we may feel disoriented. Maybe even scared. We may feel some regret about the amount of energy we have invested in the story of our favorite identity. This may be an excellent time to remind ourselves that we are part of a much greater arc of evolution. Who says we should know who we truly are now? Maybe our getting a glimpse is just perfect, so the next person that we meet or that comes after us may have an even fuller view into reality.

Being with terminally ill people, I have gotten a glimpse of what it's like to live without identity. My Uncle Gerrit, once the second-biggest greenhouse farmer in the Netherlands, was for a big part of his life deeply invested in his identity of being the rich one, the jet-setter, and special in some sort of way. He was diagnosed with cancer at age sixty-two, and died nine months after the initial diagnosis. A few months before his death, he told me two things that point me toward the reality of who we may be, beyond all our identities. First, he said, "I know the love I have for my family will stay, even when I am no longer here." A few weeks later he shared, "If life has been this much of an adventure, how much greater of an adventure will death be?" When I relax my surface stories about who I am, I connect to a sense of presence, peace, love, joy, even fascination for this moment. Thank you, Uncle Gerrit, for passing on your wisdom.

Living and leading from this deeper place, I don't need much of anything, besides making sure that the basic physical needs are met. And living from this place, which is not about protecting any identity, I am simply here. I can simply be here and be of service to what is.

Letting go of our identities, we become available to truly lead. The word *lead* is related to the Middle English word "leith," which means "die." If we let our attachments to our identities die, a much wider, interconnected sense of self may come online, which we can call unconditional love, presence, peace, joy. From this place, we naturally serve without needing to be seen to be of service. We naturally go about our day, without needing any validation. We are here, love, loved, and loving, and that is enough.

---

## Leadership Practice

*What is your favorite identity? Thank this identity for all the ways it has helped you in your life and leadership so far.*

*Who would you be if you loosened your attachment to this identity? Don't try to let it go all at once. Just experiment with loosening your attachment to who you had believed you were. See what happens. See what happens with your sense of peace, enjoyment, and capacity to truly be of service.*

# PRACTICE 30
## Letting Fear Go, Letting Reality In

IF WE GIVE our crocodilian fear a finger, it will try to take the whole hand. Fear wants to take over, feeding us the illusion that in its hands we will be safe and in control. Afraid that people might leave us, we rush in to try to say just the right thing, give them the cold shoulder first, or resort to any other manipulative coping strategy. Giving in to the fear of abandonment, we abandon ourselves and others, believing we can somehow control our experience the way we want, while in the end experiencing the opposite. No one, standing in their own two shoes, likes to be manipulated. When we give in to our fear of abandonment, we likely will experience people leaving us, tired of our crocodilian tactics.

We call this the *fear paradox*. Giving in to our fear, we behave in defensive ways, co-creating the exact result we fear the most. For example, letting our fear of hurt run our lives, we hold back, hurting ourselves and others by being inauthentic. Obsessing over our safety, we resort to quick fixes, like short-term solutions and blaming others. These forced crocodilian solutions seldom provide the long-term safety we desire.

The crocodile lives in constant opposition to reality. It wants to keep us safe by controlling our lives. Our crocodile believes that fear will help us control our experience, not trusting that the experience itself is trustworthy. Last night, I was home while some friends of mine were playing a game on the TV in the living room. I felt my fear of not having the perfect quiet evening take over. Soon, I had thoughts of wanting to force the game to end. I was considering whether to unplug the device or to create a scene by "teaching" them how what they were doing was somehow not spiritual. Fortunately, I had enough awareness not to resort to these control strategies. Instead, I chose to take a walk with another friend and enjoyed the quiet of the evening outside. Afterwards,

I decided to spend some more time with my friends in the living room. I kept noticing my alarm clock sitting on the dinner table. I needed it to get up early in the morning, before everyone else, to do my "spiritual" practices. Sitting still in the living room, I gradually started seeing how much everyone was enjoying themselves, laughing together—especially the kids were having a great time. Still, I couldn't shake my indignant feelings. One of my friends asked what was going on with me and I told him that I wasn't quite sure what to do with my feelings, but that I was annoyed they were playing the game and that I was feeling frustrated. I also said that I hesitated to talk about my feelings, as I didn't feel I had processed them adequately. My friend responded, "Thank you for sharing your feelings. I really appreciate it when you share them as they come up. That makes it a lot easier for me to relate to you." Something in me relaxed. I felt safe and included again, part of the whole.

Reflecting on this experience now, I see how it teaches exactly what I want to write about—how to release fear. Fear by its nature wants to control. It's a control energy. How do we free ourselves from fear?

It starts with acknowledging that we *have* fear. Without that, we *become* the fear, which leaves no time and attention for, no awareness of, anything else. Seeing the fear will not make it go away. In fact, it may start to become more aggressive in the horror stories that it tries to control us with—all in a last-ditch effort to bring us back in its sphere. Seeing the fear, we get to make a choice. Will we continue to give in to this fear by acting on it, or by analyzing it to death—another control strategy of the crocodile?

How would our essence—unconditional love and presence—want us to choose? It knows we are free now. Why spend another second being enmeshed with the fear? This doesn't mean the fear will just go away. It has gotten its tentacles into our nervous system, creating all kinds of fear-based chemical reactivity that may last a while longer. Choosing freedom now may not feel good in the moment.

Last night, I was unwittingly guided by life to choose another way. The universe, in the form of a friend, asked me to reveal what was going on. And then didn't demand an explanation. Very simply, the universe, in the form of my friend, let me know that he was okay being with me and my fearful reactivity. My friend didn't run away. He simply was abiding with me in the experience. Feeling held this way helped me to stop going in circles in my head. I relaxed and gave it over.

This is the other choice we have when we meet an aspect of fear. We can simply say to ourselves: I am here. I let you go now, fear, to be with my friend.

Whatever your friend may be—nature, God, Buddha, Higher Power—it doesn't matter. We simply surrender our fear into the healing presence of the universe.

## Leadership Practice

*Think of a fear you have now. How does giving in to the fear co-create exactly the result you fear the most?*

*What happens when you simply give the fear over to the universe, no longer needing to act on it, even analyze it?*

*Then what freedom and ease comes online in you?*

# PART 4

## Enjoying Balance

# PRACTICE 31
## Finding Balance

NIGHT AND DAY, hot and cold, rain and sun, winter and summer, male and female—nature seems to always balance itself out. Even during a fierce thunderstorm, we can sense the clear skies that are coming. And in the midst of winter, we sense the summer in the rising morning sun.

The word *balance* comes from the Latin word *bilanx*, which means "scale pans." Balance requires the coming together of opposites. From our crocodile's tunnel vision we only see one extreme at a time—it's light or dark, good or bad, right or wrong. Holding the complexity of both coexisting is too much for the primitive part of our nervous system. Our crocodile needs to control our experience now, even if it means hanging out in one extreme of seeing or behaving. Allowing for natural balance to occur is not part of its repertoire.

In our heart, we naturally hold complexity. Our physical heart balances out the body—being one organ, with a right and left chamber, helping our blood course through our veins with its rhythmic pulse. From the heart of our being, we hold complexity from a place of silence, watching things naturally fall into place.

Eastern wisdom teaches us about balance in two words: *yin* and *yang*—yin pointing to our intuitive, connecting side, related to the right side of our brain and the left side of our body; and yang symbolizing the purposeful, firm side, related to the left side of our brain and the right side of our body. We know when we are in balance. We feel in flow; we naturally take care of things, go about our day, and don't get stuck in any particular experience. Like cooking, we mix purposefulness with connectedness and intuition with drive into a wholesome combination of energies that nourishes us and those we are with.

When the crocodile notices we're off balance, it will rush in to fix it from a place of fear, with either controlling or pleasing, lower-yang or lower-yin strategies. With the yang side weaker, we may experience difficulty moving toward our goals and purpose. Our lower-yang crocodile believes that micromanaging, making others wrong, rushing to an answer, trying to rescue, beating others, and doing things perfectly will get us to the safe balance it craves. Our lower-yin crocodile may seem more caring, but it is just as destructive. It will try to force the hand of life by manipulating, pleasing, cajoling, dramatizing, or posturing as the martyr in the situation.

With a yin deficit, we may have the experience of feeling distant from others, not having the meaningful relationships we want and need to feel whole and to be effective. Our lower-yin crocodile will try to get the relationships it is desperate about back on track through manipulation, pleasing, and any of the other strategies we discussed above. Whatever does the job, thinks the crocodile, that's the strategy I pick. Our lower-yang crocodile is not very skilled in dealing with others, let alone empathizing with them, so it focuses on the task at hand and goes into overachievement mode. It will try to produce and be perfect, hoping that someone will notice and love them because of what they did, rather than because of who they are. A somewhat more aggressive version of this lower-yang crocodile is that it will become a bully who tells people what to do, coercing them to comply with the fantasy of the relationship it is pursuing.

How do we know our lower-yang or lower-yin side has taken over? In one word: fear. We know we're no longer coming from a place of presence, peace, unconditional love, but from some kind of fear-based reaction that compulsively tries to make us safe again.

Noticing our lower-yin and lower-yang crocodiles at work gives us a choice. We can choose to slow down and take another perspective from which to approach the situation. How can I bring higher-yang energy— more purposefulness, stillness, quiet, and fortitude—to this situation? Or how can I become more empathic, open, understanding, and accepting of those around me, practicing higher-yin relationship building?

The crocodile will make balance and everything else into a self-accumulation and self-improvement project, thinking that a better me will be more lovable and therefore safer. From the ground of our essence, we can see our balancing efforts with different eyes. What if every imbalance became an opportunity for us to get to know more of our higher-yang and higher-yin sides? And what if it also became an opportunity to extend these energies to others?

---

## Leadership Practice

*Notice where you go naturally first: being purposeful, still, more rational, possibly more task-focused—higher yang? Or do you find yourself more comfortable deeply connecting to others, being empathic and open, deeply sensing what the truth of them and the situation is—higher yin?*

*In what situations do you see opportunities to rebalance your yin and yang sides?*

# PRACTICE 32
## Yang Resolve

M Y CROCODILE'S REPERTOIRE for working with life seems vast yet is very limited. The crocodile comes up with countless variations on the same theme: How can I protect myself from egoic death? Or in one word: fear. Listening to the voice of the crocodile is like listening to some news stations all day long. Never a shortage in supply of the next horror story, yet all saying the same thing: Life is dangerous and we should be on edge, always.

Giving in to crocodilian stories, we miss out on a very different frequency we can operate from. Tuning in to higher yang and yin—both radio stations broadcasting unconditional love—we discover strength we didn't know we had, humor we thought belonged only to other people, a lightness of being that is deeply compassionate and wise, a deep sense of interconnectedness with others, and a gentleness towards all of us, rooted in an atmosphere of peace and unconditional love. And these are only a few pointers to what our experience may be when we commit to operating from a different frequency.

Just as the morning starts with the rising of the sun, announcing a new day, we similarly can open ourselves to unconditional love becoming our lived experience by being intentional about it. Since for most of us our crocodilian momentum is so well practiced, it requires an inner resolve in us to step out of this fearful stream of thinking and feeling. Setting a strong intention to tame our crocodiles and come from a higher place is not a one-time deal; it's an ongoing practice.

Being intentional is associated with our higher-yang energy. We allow ourselves to become very still and ask: What is really the most important thing in my life? What do I really wish to commit myself to in my life, today? I can see what I am in fact committed to by looking at how I spend my time and attention. How much time and effort do I spend dwelling on fearful thoughts and emotions? How much of my action comes from this fearful place? How much am I living and leading from a place of truth and unconditional love, or whatever is most important to me in life?

What's most important to you is not a trivial question. It may require some dedicated time and attention to help you become clear about what's really most important to you. Keep an eye out for the guilt crocodile, who wants to tell you how rotten, bad, and dysfunctional you've been so far. Don't fall for this thinking—it's simply the crocodile trying to protect its hold on your life by trying to weaken your resolve to look at truth. The crocodile, like any other system, will fight for its own survival, no matter how destructive it may be for the larger system. The crocodile prioritizes small personhood over our larger purpose.

Contemplating what's most important to you can become like a root that grows deeper and deeper the more you water it with your time and attention. Contemplating the question in and of itself may bring you a sense of joy and the deepening of an inner resolve to focus your life's energy on what's most important to you and let go of any distractions.

Once we have greater clarity on our purpose, we may stretch ourselves by asking: On a scale from 1 to 10, how much am I committed to my purpose?—for example, of loving myself and others unconditionally, of being truthful, of being humble, or of whatever is the purpose that makes your heart sing.

If your self-assessment is less than 10, what would make it a 10? What stories that you tell yourself—or to be more precise, the crocodilian stories you listen to—are keeping you from a 10? Maybe you tell yourself that you don't have the strength to live your purpose. Is that true? Who would you be without that thought? Or maybe you think you don't know how to live your purpose yet? Ok, is that true? What is the smallest step you can take right now to live your purpose a little bit more?

Rooted in the inner resolve to live our purpose, no matter what, life becomes an adventure. With a purpose in our heart and mind, we start our day with an inspiring assignment: How can I live more of my purpose today? How can I bring it into my work? My commute? My interactions with others? My care of self? Notice how the crocodile sees everything as a means to get its needs met. Living and leading from intention, we greet every moment with the mindset of a samurai—how can I bring all of my true self here and use this moment as an opportunity to grow in my capacity to be my intention, to give to others from my intention, and to do my best, undeterred by any pain and hallucinations that the crocodile may try to distract me with?

## Leadership Practice

*Contemplate what is most important to you in life. What would happen if you dedicated even more of your time and attention to it?*

*How would you lead differently to the challenge that has been given to you today?*

## PRACTICE 33
### Opening to Being a Yin Embrace

WHAT DO YOU allow yourself to be held by? What do you rest in? Our crocodile is always scurrying around, looking for the next thing to find security in. Did I get this done? How did they like it? Will I get it done? Will they like it? The crocodile keeps striving for a score in life it feels comfortable with. It approaches life and leadership as a project it believes we'll get graded on. Tellingly, the words *score* and *scare* have only one letter difference. We can scare ourselves into continuously striving for more, hoping we somehow will get that score that will make us feel happy and safe.

Scoring is a big part of our society—we receive grades in school, and we track our fitness levels, our health indicators, our credit score, our bank account, the number of followers we have online, and how much people approve of us and our actions—we score even our own mental states. This is not to say these scores don't have a place. They can be helpful gauges to tell us what needs care now.

However, our crocodile derives a lot more meaning from our scores than just information to help us focus. It tries to find safety in scoring by constructing our identity based upon it, like: I am a good person, I am enough, I am respected, I am competent, and I am wise and compassionate. Driven by the identity of "I am a good person," I may not say my truth when I sense it may offend someone. Under the influence of the idea of being competent, I may become less willing to try something new. Believing that I am compassionate, I may become less willing to look at all the ways I am not yet that. Our identities limit our growth and are unstable. Life continues to throw us challenges that tell us: you are not that, that, or that. We can't find lasting peace and security in our identities, however high we may score on any given day.

So where do we find peace and security that we can rely on, maybe even a sense of warmth? I sometimes wake up anxious in the morning. The act of simply getting up and meditating for a while usually helps me to let go of some of my anxiety and rest in this present moment. In this present moment, I have no problems. In this present moment I am simply here. In this present moment, I am nobody in particular. I am simply here. In this present moment, I can surrender to the present moment. In this present moment, I can relax and open. In this present moment, I can open to life and everything in it. This may seem scary. Paradoxically, the more I let go of this present moment, the more I experience what's left after I let it all go. What's left—and I mean what's really left—is not scary at all. It's the place that goes even beyond fear. It's the place that is not scared, even when I am scared; that is not anxious when I am; that is not excited when I feel it. It's the place that lies underneath my emotions and thoughts and at the same time includes all emotions and thoughts.

Surrendering to this moment, I get to know more of the essence of who I truly am. I may also start to experience the unconditionally caring aspects of my true self—like feeling held, feeling peace, and feeling unconditional love. Knowing at a deeper and deeper level that I am unconditionally cared for helps calm my anxiety. I connect with my true mother, the one who holds me no matter what, who makes no demands on me, who is infinitely compassionate and is simply there for me, always.

Resting in the embrace of my true self, I heal, I relax, I become more playful. Feeling secure in the embrace of my true self, I no longer keep making demands on my external environment to help me feel secure. I no longer keep score not to be scared.

Resting in the embrace of my true self, I learn to extend that unconditional embrace to others. I am simply here for them. I am present to them, fully, with all their emotions, and all crocodiles included. I don't have to fix anything, as I know they also can rest in the embrace of true self. This is not something someone else can give you. It's something we all get to experience and find out for ourselves.

Resting in the true embrace, we embrace ourselves and others as we are. I remember this embrace as the great caring yin energy that is available to me and anyone else, at all times. All we have to do is to drop our protection strategies and open up to this moment. Then the moment comes to greet us. As we embrace this moment, this moment embraces us.

---

## Leadership Practice

*Allow yourself to stop what you are doing for a moment and become completely present to this moment. Open your heart to this moment. Feel how this moment tries to embrace you. Open some more and simply experience how you are held, no matter what. Constantly.*

## PRACTICE 34
### From the Rocks into the River

OUR CROCODILE WANTS everything to be lined up perfectly all the time to match its expectations of what is safe. Its go-to strategy to make this happen is control—diverting our yang strength from taking care of what is needed to overdoing, striving to keep our fragile sense of identity intact. As we will discuss in practice #35, it also uses yin energy to control, for example through manipulation, drama, and other forms of seduction.

Our crocodile believes it can win the fight against reality. If only I have enough money, then I will be able to buy my way to freedom, comfort, and specialness. If only I get this job done on time, then I will feel safe. If only I know that this will happen, then everything will be ok. Our crocodile keeps us very busy striving to attain a perfect world that we'll never reach.

My family is currently in the middle of moving cities. My controlling, lower-yang crocodile has a field day with this. It wants to know when we'll move, what house we'll live in, how it will all work out financially, what furniture will go where, where my clients will come from, and who will take care of the garden and the pool when we're not home. And this is only a smidgeon of the to-do list that my crocodile is obsessing about. All of these questions have merit. It's just that the crocodile wants to force certainty now.

It does so by trying to convince me to overpay on the house we like so we can close the deal, trying to force me and my partner to complete everything today, and rush the moving date so I don't have to be in this in-between time of uncertainty any longer.

Come to think of it, our move is a wonderful opportunity to help me let go of some of my controlling beliefs and behaviors that disconnect me from the flow of life. Who would I be without the need to control everything? What would become possible for me?

This in-between time then becomes a time to deepen my commitment to being who I truly am—the ground of being that is not attached to any circumstances. Letting go of my need to control, I start to access a sense of stillness inside of me that helps me stay strong and focused, taking care of whatever is needed now. Letting go of my need for things to work exactly the way I hoped, I open myself to things being the way they are. Letting go of my sense of self-importance, as if I am the center of the universe that controls everything, I get out of life's business and focus more on my part in it.

For the crocodile, letting go is very scary. It wants to force me to stay in control, no matter what happens, because it doesn't trust what happens when I don't. It only trusts what it controls. I sense our move is in one way a small preparation for the big letting-go that we all get to do, letting go of this life. Dare I stand on the doorstep of infinity now, living moment to moment, deeply feeling into what is needed now?

The more I let go, the deeper the sense of peace is that I access. Paradoxically, the more I let go of my need to control how my physical home shapes up to be, the more I feel at home now. Maybe this whole move is simply yet another way to help me find my way closer to my true home?

Maybe the crocodile's incessant drive for control, for trying to help me to feel stable at home is simply a fear-based interpretation of a deep yearning we all share, which is to feel at peace, at home with ourselves and our world? This calling to be home is so deep, and our crocodile is trying to find shortcuts by trying to control our outside circumstances to get us there: the perfect job, home, partner, health, even mental state.

Looking at my life, I see how much energy this controlling crocodile chews up and how rigid it makes me. It takes all the adventure, meaning, beauty, and connection out of my experience. Who would I be without the need to control? Would I still be able to take care of things? Of course, presence, innate wisdom, knows what to do, like the river knows its way around the rocks.

My job is to get more into the river and less into the business of trying to move the rocks. The more I am the river, the more things flow.

The more I try to move the rocks, the more I exhaust myself and others around me, by trying to do a task that is not mine. The more I stay in my business and let life take care of its business, the more serene and at home I feel.

———

## Leadership Practice

*Think of something you try to control. How is it working for you? How is it similar to trying to move rocks in the river?*


*What would happen if you allowed yourself to become more like the river as you approach the challenge you are facing?*

## PRACTICE 35
## Clean Warmth or a Hot Mess?

WHEN I THINK of warmth, I think of my Aunt Durkje Kleefstra. She passed away more than twenty years ago but I still remember the warmth she shared with me. Being with her, my family and I felt at home. She had such warm hands, and her eyes were oh so gentle. I remember her coming to visit the farm where we lived. Whenever she would show up in the driveway, we kids would run toward the car and embrace her. She had a magnetic presence, radiating warmth.

Another friend and leader who comes to mind is René Yoakum. She currently serves as the Chief Customer and People Officer at Remitly, a financial services company. Whenever she is in a meeting, things feel different—she brings, besides sharp intellect and many other leadership skills, a sense of warmth and shared humanity into the room.

We have such a capacity, like Durkje and Rene, to lead with warmth. Stop for a moment and sense the warmth that comes through your heart area. Let it expand and radiate throughout your whole body and then fill the room where you are now. Our yin-ability to connect, to extend human warmth, to connect deeply to each other and ourselves, is such an amazing part of being human.

As with all parts, our fear-based crocodile diverts our yin-warmth to its own self-protective purposes. It uses our warmth as a shield and as a weapon. It pleases, seduces, blames, gossips, gives unwanted advice, predicts negative outcomes, poses as a martyr, retreats into an ivory tower, and anything else it can think of to enmesh its environment. The lower-yin crocodile is the star in its own drama that can make your head spin. Giving into the manipulation of lower yin, you may feel you lose your sense of purpose; you forget who you are, what you stand for, and what is true. This is exactly the purpose of the lower-yin energy—it uses everyone as a parasite, for its own survival.

It abuses our beautiful capacity to share warmth and creates a hot mess. Being in this hot mess gives it a sense of power. Sometimes we may resort to lower-yin strategies when our higher-yang purposeful power is not readily available to us. Afraid to assert our purpose cleanly, we go about it in a roundabout way. We resort to indirectness, and sometimes seduction. We say one thing but have a secret agenda. With everything we do, we try to put our tentacles into the other, trying to get them to do what we are afraid to ask directly. Wanting to go somewhere, we may ask the other person, "Do you want to go here?" with a sheepish smile, as opposed to asserting that we would like to go and asking the other person to join us.

Why is lower-yin energy so hard to give up for many of us? It gives us a sense of control. Manipulating others gives us a false sense of strength. We feel we somehow will get our way through the backdoor, even if it means we are out of integrity with our highest self.

Remember the crocodile is *only* interested in our survival. That's why, after a manipulation has succeeded, we may feel good for a moment. "We did it!" the crocodile celebrates. In the meantime, our wiser being watches and sees it differently. We may feel a sense of unease after we have been manipulating for a while. Our lack of ease can be like a whisper that wants us to wake up: "How do you really want to be, coming from your true essence?"

We tame our lower-yin crocodile by naming it. Simply calling out our own emotional enmeshment strategies weakens their hold over us. In the space we create, we can take a few deep breaths into the belly and reflect: How do I really wish to approach this?

We don't throw the baby out with the bathwater. We don't need to go from warm enmeshment to cold purposefulness. We can be assertive *and* warm. Imagine what becomes possible in your conversations, in your work, and for your sense of fulfillment when you practice higher-yang clarity and higher-yin clean warmth. Your crocodile may want to recreate lots more episodes of emotional drama with you in the center. Instead, you can clear the air and share the clean warmth of your heart with yourself and with everyone you meet today.

## Leadership Practice

*Think of a person, maybe like my Aunt Durkje, or my friend Rene, who role models clean warmth for you. What can you learn from them?*

*Where can you see evidence of potential enmeshment in your relationships? How could you be more assertive AND warm in this relationship?*

# PRACTICE 36
## Sky-like Presence

OUR CROCODILES NEVER rest. What do I need to do to be safe now? What could I get so I shore up my self-image a bit more? What are some quick fixes that make me feel better now? What should I worry about today? The crocodile provides endless content for us to stay busy with. The crocodile keeps us in a perennial state of imbalance. We may even find ourselves off balance as we practice higher-yang purposefulness and higher-yin connectedness. We can become so purposeful that we momentarily lose our connection with others. And we can get so deeply connected with others that we disconnect from the larger purpose. Our inner landscape tends to go off balance. Where can we find more lasting stability?

Take a moment and take a few deep breaths into the belly. Allow yourself to become deeply present to this moment, sky-like awareness, peace, being. Presence is always here, no matter what thoughts, feelings, and actions occur. Presence—our awareness—is like the sky, or the screen within which and upon which the cloud-like images of thoughts, feelings, and actions occur. The sky doesn't mind what happens within it. It's fine with puffy clouds, thunderclouds, tornadoes, and everything in between. Similarly, when we rest in presence, even *as* presence, we become sky-like. We become the context within which the content of our experiences occurs. The context doesn't change. The content does all the time. Resting as the context, we connect to the constancy of who we are. Identifying with the content, we get lost. We have comfortable and uncomfortable moments that we translate into us being comfortable and uncomfortable. The sky, our true essence, is beyond uncomfortable and comfortable. It includes all of our experiences, yet doesn't identify with or dwell on any of them. The sky, who we are, is free from experiences, yet includes all of them. The sky doesn't make any demands. It simply is. It is just as much here on a sunny as on a stormy day.

Resting as presence may seem impractical, and yet it may be the most practical thing we can do. How do we get things done when we rest as the sky? Let's first examine what happens when we don't rest as the sky.

We can get so caught up in any one experience that we forget about the rest. We procrastinate, perfect, please, manipulate, try to be special, or engage in any other crocodilian pastime to get us to an experience we believe will make us feel safe and loved. This takes tremendous amounts of energy. Our crocodile is a huge energy consumer.

Let's look at how our day unfolds resting as presence. First, as presence we may become aware of our body. We become grounded in our body and rooted in ourselves. We can evoke more of some of the aspects of presence—you could say to experience the sky as the sky—by using our body as a portal. Resting our awareness on the sits bones, and relaxing into our seat, we may experience a sense of spaciousness that is boundless, infinite, at rest. Moving our attention up our torso to the heart center, resting our attention there, we may experience the sky as being alive, light, even having a sense of warmth. Whatever experience you have of the present heart, stay there for a little bit to let yourself feel and remember. Then move your attention to the area between your eyebrows, your third eye. From that place, the sky may be experienced as clear, with insights into what is true now. Enjoy the clarity of being that may emerge as you rest there.

Consider these aspects: space, warmth, and clarity. What would it be like if you could be these three and bring them more to every moment today? How practical is that? From a sense of spaciousness, we participate in our tasks and conversations without getting stuck in them, yet fully giving ourselves to them, not needing to shy away from anything, as the sky's space contains everything. From the warmth of the sky, we may infuse our work with compassion and understanding for ourselves and others, enjoying the warmth that comes through us. From third eye clarity, we become discerning, knowing what to do and what to say and what not.

Being as the sky, we stay in balance, even when our thoughts and feelings are in a momentary stormy episode. Being as the sky, we rest, even in the middle of a hurricane. We demand nothing, yet are clear about our standards. We become more interested in giving than receiving, as we, the sky, are already full. We are free to give, as we can't lose who we are. And we have no fear of change, because who we are in essence remains unchanged.

---

## Leadership Practice

*Take a moment and allow yourself to become really present. Take a few conscious breaths into the belly. Then rest your attention on the sits bones—allow yourself to feel the spaciousness of your being. Then rest your attention on the heart center—connect with the warmth of your being. Finally, travel up to the third eye center—enjoy the clarity of who you are.*

*Please note that these words are only pointers to how you may experience who you are. Stay true to your own experience. You are the only one who can decide what is true about you.*

## PRACTICE 37
### Doing Nothing

THE HARDEST THING to do is often to do absolutely nothing. Allow yourself, for today, a few moments of doing absolutely nothing. Be like the blank page you see in front of you. Notice what becomes possible for you when you give yourself permission to do absolutely nothing. Drop all technique. Just be here now.

## *Leadership Practice*

*Do absolutely nothing for a few minutes. Just be here.*

# PRACTICE 38
## Finding the Balance We Always Are

IF YOU'RE ANYTHING like me, you get out of balance multiple times a day. The other day I was in a meeting with a client to talk about some possible new team development work. I am also in the midst of signing papers for a new home. And even though I can easily afford this purchase, part of my energy said: You've got to close this new deal to help pay for your mortgage! This thinking felt uncomfortable and for a little while distracted me from being 100 percent present in the meeting.

When I noticed that my crocodile had taken over my mind, I was upset at first. Oh no, why had I given in to this crocodilian scarcity thinking again?! I should be present, darn it, I was failing at being my authentic self! Yes, my crocodile is crafty. If worrying over an outcome doesn't do it, maybe having me run after the "I-should-be-present-or-else" self-image might do the job. When we're off balance, our crocodile does things that push us even further off balance.

We regain balance by remembering that who we truly are is always in balance. Presence, unconditional love, the peace that we are, is always in balance, even when another part of us may be creating havoc. In these moments of crocodilian-induced imbalance, it may seem impossible to find our balance again. Our crocodile will slyly keep feeding us all kinds of ways to keep us from being present. For the crocodile, having us be in a state of anxious imbalance is preferred. It thinks, when we're off balance, at least we're on guard, and offense seems to be the best defense to protect us from ego-death. The crocodile will have us work hard to keep it together, by having us self-punish; overanalyze; please others to get back into their good graces; manipulate; claim the center of attention as the Special One, the Martyr, or the Rescuer; and micromanage ourselves and others.

Relaxing and letting go is anathema for our crocodile. The crocodile keeps our time and attention trapped in a fruitless struggle to get to balance. It never works. Because the balance we are cannot be achieved. It simply is. We cannot earn love, we are love. We cannot earn peace, we are peace.

In the cacophony of crocodilian voices, how do we remember this, especially when we're triggered and our anxious crocodiles literally take our breath away?

Breathing deeply into our belly and placing our attention there for a while helps. The crocodile overuses our head. It sometimes literally makes our head hurt by overthinking, obsessing, worrying, and trying to control. Placing our attention on the breathing in our belly diverts our attention to a whole other part of our being that goes beyond our thinking mind. Over time, what we withdraw our attention from withers, as does our crocodilian thinking. By placing our attention on our breathing, we nourish a calmer part of ourselves that can be a doorway to us experiencing more deeply who we truly are.

Adding a mantra to this self-balancing exercise can help too. "I am love, loved, and lovable" is a great one to help reclaim our senses. Repeat this a few times now: "I am love, loved, and lovable." Notice what happens with your sense of balance. You may experience some relaxation, letting go of the crocodilian struggle for control and safety. We orient toward our essence, being love. We find real safety in that. Not the pseudo-safety of having circumstances or people validate our self-images. Validation and self-images come and go and are inherently unstable. No, the safety that comes from resting in who we always are, is always here. This essence doesn't need propping up through performance or validation. It's simply here.

In the client meeting the other day, I remembered breathing and letting go of my thinking, even though I didn't get as far as reminding myself that I was love. Relaxing, I became quiet, started to talk less, and for a moment observed all of us in the room. From that place of awareness, I reconnected to why I was there—to help the client grow as leaders and as a team. I was not there to pay my mortgage payment. I will take care of that one later. Not in this meeting.

Relaxing the crocodilian self-talk helps us refocus on what is needed now. It helps us reconnect with the powerful love energy that we are and that we can bring to everything that comes our way.

---

## Leadership Practice

*How does your crocodile react when you are off balance? Does it try to push you into guilt, other forms of self-criticism, overworking, overanalyzing, pleasing, withdrawal, manipulating, being the special one, martyrdom, micromanagement, rigid thinking, drama, or something else? Take note of your go-to crocodilian reaction to imbalance.*


*Who would you be without this crocodilian reaction? Practice rebalancing now by breathing deeply into the belly and repeating the mantra: "I am love, loved, and lovable," three times. Take a moment to reflect on your experience.*

# PRACTICE 39
## Accepting Our Experience

MY CROCODILE DREAMS that one day all my problems will be gone, life will be just the way I want it, and I will be happy. Pursuing this fairy tale can be so alluring. Our movies, advertisements, even our schooling points us there. We are conditioned to believe that we can earn the good life.

Giving in to this belief of the good life we can earn, we keep working hard, harder and harder, until life tells us to stop. At some point our health, our relationships, and our inner experiences don't add up to the formula, "If I keep working harder I will have a good life." Of course, there is a place for working hard. It can be necessary and even enjoyable. However, it's the fantasy part of the good life in the future that causes us pain. Hoping for the good life, we don't take time to enjoy this moment. Thinking we've finally arrived at our good life, we close ourselves off from the fullness of life, including mental and emotional pain, sickness, and death.

"Do we continuously have to deny our experience?" my teacher Adyashanti once asked. In the pursuit of love, peace, and joy, we can develop a fantasy that those things are over there and that we are over here. Or, if we experience something that looks like love, peace, and joy, we want to hold on to it. If even the slightest trace of sadness, anger, or anxiety enters our consciousness, we flat-out deny it.

As a child, I loved being on the beach. One day while I was there with my aunt, she asked me, "Why do you make this big sand wall around your towel?" It seemed like a silly question to me. I always built a big sand wall around my towel, like a sea dike protecting me from everything around me. Why wouldn't I? As an adult, I kept building sea dikes around me, not on the beach, but in my life. At some point, I had become so scared of life that I wanted to become a monk and retreat behind the cloister walls. Truth be told, I also wanted to deepen my spiritual practices there. That was also part of my motivation. I didn't enter the monastery, but I kept building walls to protect me from outside influences. I would not talk to certain people in my workshops, afraid of what they might say. I would tell myself I *had to* meditate thirty minutes in the morning in order to be able to do my work. Waking up with anxiety would mean that I failed and couldn't do my work that day, and my partner, family, and friends would have to behave exactly according to my peace, joy, and love plan; otherwise I'd throw them out. I thought I was doing all I could to create a peaceful life.

Instead, I was at war with life. I was in a constant battle with my experience. I had shifted my micromanagement tendencies to my having the perfect experience, so I could feel I was doing my spiritual path perfectly.

Making peace with life is radical and an ongoing practice for me. Making peace with life invites me to let go of any and *all* expectations I place on life, others, and myself. Making peace with life means that I accept things exactly as they are—this includes accepting my likes and my dislikes. The more I accept life, the more I experience the fullness of life. The more I experience the fullness of life, the less I separate myself from it and the more I am at one with it. The more I am at one with it, the more insight I gain into what is really happening now and what is needed. And the more insight I have, the easier it becomes to love everything, as I see things more for what they are and less for what my expectations want them to be.

From the eyes of acceptance, an anxious client turns into a person who experiences some discomfort, and who, just like me, wants to be happy. I can be present to them, and extend loving attention, without having to fix anything, as I can also see that the only way people will come back to peace is by finding that in themselves.

From the eyes of acceptance, a sense of anxiety in myself becomes simply a pocket of energy that is there for now. It's not me and yet it is with me for the moment. I can be with it as I would be with a guest: attentive, without getting lost in it. "I had a hard time with this," I will tell a counselor. She will ask me to talk about it briefly, after which she'll ask, "And so, what are you going to do with the rest of your day?" I find this so healing. From the eyes of acceptance, I can see things for what they are. I don't confuse anxiety with the essence of who I am. Anxiety doesn't deserve my complete attention all day long. I can simply be with it for a while, as it's only a small, temporary guest in my being, and move on.

Life is here now. Just as it is. Anything in us that doesn't want that is us putting something between us and life. That separation hurts. True joy comes from accepting totally what is, without any expectations of what should be. In a state of acceptance, we see clearly. We also see clearly how life takes care of itself. Yes, this includes our being nudged to do our part. In a state of acceptance, we are more able to listen to what we are called to do now and what is not ours to do.

Accepting life as it is, we become life—the endless mystery for which there are no words.

---

## Leadership Practice

*What expectations do you put on how today should go? Who would you be without these expectations?*

*What happens when you accept yourself, others, and life a bit more? Then what becomes possible for you?*

## PRACTICE 40
### Joining Balance

Life seems to be in balance whether we are in balance with it or not. Every day starts with a new dawn. The sun rises, flowers open, we reach noon, and soon we're going into dusk and the rest of the evening. Spring comes after winter, summer after spring, fall after summer, and winter after fall. We are born, we grow up, some of us have children, we live life, a new generation grows up, and we die. The more I study life, the more I am in awe of the balancing act it is and has been for eons.

How can we join life in its balancing act? Giving ourselves fully to this moment helps. Maybe you have experienced dancing, and completely losing yourself in it. Or, perhaps you have been in a conversation with your teammates where you were so much in the moment, engrossed in what you were doing, that time just flew by. Maybe you have taken a walk and been overcome by the beauty of it all. Or, possibly, you have addressed a challenge where you felt that you were carried by some higher power, just knowing what to say and when, with no regrets, right on the mark.

To find balance we need to let go, as a tightrope walker does, of any thinking and action that gets us out of balance. We are in balance, like the tightrope walker, when we become very still on the inside and in harmony with this moment. We are in balance when we play our part completely, without worrying about other people playing theirs. We are like the violinist in an orchestra who becomes her melody, joining the sounds and rhythms around her and within her completely.

Crocodilian thinking interferes with our balance. The crocodile doubts whether we can handle balance. It's afraid we might lose its precious possession—our emotional identity. To find balance, we need to be willing to give up all our identities. Attachment to our identities keeps us out of balance. If I think I should be a nice person, I put this nice person between me and reality, closing myself off from seeing truth as it is, and curtailing my options to respond only as the "nice" one would. If I believe I should be a competent person, I cut myself off from a vast amount of reality, totally putting my balance at risk, as I won't easily admit areas where I am not skilled. Believing that I should be perfect, I disappear in the fog of this crocodilian fantasy, and disconnect from life as it is. Life is perfect in its imperfection, just like I am perfect in my imperfection. I am life. Believing that I am separate from life, with my own ideas of who I am, I get out of balance, trying to fix life and myself to comply with my expectations. We all know how well this works. When we believe we are the director of the play of life, we sign up for mayhem. People and events won't comply with our expectations—not even our own bodies and minds like to be controlled. They will do what's in balance for them, not what we think should be in balance for them.

How do we find balance then? By letting go of any and all thinking about who we and life should be. By completely being here now. Not being here now tied to our agendas of what should happen, but ready to be with this moment. Ready to pounce on it, if called for. Or to caress it, or...

Life will tell us. If the tightrope walker tries to stick to his agenda of what should happen and who he should be, he will fall. He doesn't control the wind, the moisture, even what his emotions may do while on the rope. What he can focus on is being completely in this moment and let a power come through him—you can call this intuition, or higher order—to guide him what to do and when.

We can walk our tightrope anytime. Sitting down to do email in the morning, we may take a deep breath and ask our heart: What am I called to focus on now? What must I take care of now? What can wait till later? How do I want to be while addressing these emails? What energy do I want to bring to them? Having a conversation with a colleague, we may notice our crocodile if it comes up and let it go, without worrying about it. The only thing we really need to do is to let it go, so we can be completely here in this moment, with this other person, focused on the task at hand. Preparing a presentation, we may ask: What is this really for? What intention can I set for this presentation that is in balance with myself, the people I am serving, and the task at hand? Let your intuition guide you. Start walking now and remember, it's one step at a time. Take it easy. Life doesn't rush from dawn to dusk. It takes a whole day to get there. Join life in its rhythm today and enjoy the balance that you are.

---

## Leadership Practice

*Take a moment to reflect on a part of nature that you love. How is it in balance? What can you learn from it to bring balance today?*

# PART 5

## Finding Truth

# PRACTICE 41
## True Freedom

Is IT TRUE that you should work hard? Is it true that they shouldn't judge you? Is it true that you should get what you want today? Reflect on these questions for a moment. You may find some lightness as you let go of any preconceived notions about what reality is and what it is not. It also can be unsettling to examine our beliefs for truth. We may discover that what we believe was true really isn't.

The word *true* stems, among others, from old Frisian *trywe* and Dutch *getrouw*, which means being faithful to. Being truthful, we are faithful to reality. We are loyal to what is true. Now, what is true, really?

Let's do a test. Ask yourself how old you are. Answer honestly. My answer today is that I am forty-seven years old. Now respond to this question again, but now respond with a little lie. I lie that I am forty-five years old. What do you notice? What difference do you notice between telling truth versus a lie? Chances are you feel a sense of peace, maybe even stillness, when you speak truth. And you may feel some inner unrest telling yourself a lie, even if it's a little one. Somehow, deep down, we know what is true, and what is not. We can use our capacity to discern truth to become more genuine leaders. Instead of unconsciously believing the beliefs we once picked up somewhere, we are ready to question everything for truth.

Consider the following beliefs. How does it feel when you say these to yourself? I should be perfect. I should please others. I should do what's expected. I should be competent. I should be nice. I should know the answer. I should control the outcome. I should never hurt anyone. I should always be clear. I should be special.

How does it feel to give energy to any one of these beliefs? Likely, giving attention to any of these beliefs feels heavy, possibly destabilizing,

135

even though some of these beliefs may be familiar to you. Likely your crocodiles hold some of them as true, as they are quite common.

Now pick a belief from the list that rings true to your crocodile. For me that belief is "I should do what's expected of me." How do I feel when I believe this thought? I feel heavy and uncertain, judgmental of myself for not complying with the expectations of some. I also notice some judgment toward others for not complying with my expectations of them. Now, consider this: "Can I absolutely know that it's true that I should comply with the expectations others have of me?" No, not really. Upon closer examination I see that I don't really know what others' expectations are of me. I make a lot of this up in my own mind. And even with those who have told me what they expect of me, I can see that it's not absolutely true that I should comply. I can choose to do what is asked and I can also choose not to. For example, I can choose to give in to my fearful projections of how others may react in case I don't comply, or I can let these projections go and ask my heart, my higher owl self, to guide me to wise, compassionate action. I can let my fearful crocodile or my wise owl drive my action. Letting go of the false belief that I should comply with expectations, I discover inner freedom that comes with inner self-accountability to act from the highest truth that I can see, not the mishmash of beliefs that I have picked up somewhere.

Truth has a quality of freedom and unassailability. Grounded in truth, we relieve ourselves from spending mental and emotional energy on believing, acting on, and experiencing the effects of living half-truths. Half-truths are unstable. They take a lot of mental energy to justify.

What is absolutely true? Are any of our thoughts absolutely true? Our thoughts are at best simple descriptors of reality and also manipulative storytellers that fool us when our crocodile is in charge. Is any thought absolutely true? It can't be. Our thoughts are only approximations of truth. This realization can be both freeing and disconcerting. Free from the need to have thoughts that are absolutely true, we lose our obsessive need to understand. We may tap into a lightness of being, a sense of surrender to life, to reality.

If no thought is absolutely true, not even the one you just read, then how do we orient ourselves in life? Thoughts are helpful pointers to what is true. They can be very helpful in discerning what is not true, as well. To operate with no sense of what is true would be impossibly exhausting. Our brains are wired to hold a set of assumptions and beliefs about who we are and how the world works that allow us to move through life with some ease. Many of these beliefs are largely unconscious. Observing our thoughts can give us clues as to what these conscious and unconscious beliefs might be. Once we notice these things we hold as truth, then the adventure can begin. We can use thinking to peel away the layers of half-truths, helping us come in touch with the truth of our being, which we cannot really describe in thinking. As it says in the Tao Te Ching: "The tao that can be spoken is not the true tao." We cannot describe who we are. We may be able to experience and express it. How do you describe love really? How do you conceptualize an embrace? How do you explain what peace really is?

## Leadership Practice

*Reflect on a thought that you have that bothers you. Look at it more closely. Hold it like a stone you picked up on the beach. Turn it over and examine its details. Is this thought always true? Does this thought have an energy of fear? What assumptions or beliefs does this thought imply about you, about others, about the world?*

*What would your life be like if you let go of this thought? What would it be like to hold this thought like an experiment and do some testing to see when it is really true and when it's clearly not true? Is this thought absolutely true?*

*What would it be like if you hold onto the truth of this thought with a more relaxed grip? What would it be like to let go of the thought completely? Who would you be without this thought? Then what becomes possible for you?*

## PRACTICE 42
### Spotting the Crocodilian Blockbuster Movies

OUR CROCODILE WORKS overtime, untamed, every day and night of our lives. It feeds us an ongoing stream of false stories that appear real to us: You should do this now, so you'll get or feel what you want. If you don't do this, that will happen. You are unworthy. They should be doing that and they are doing something else. This thing you are working on you may never finish. You are the best. You just have too much to do. These people aren't fair. You are a loser. You are a winner....

Our crocodilian narratives are like a newsreel that keeps updating us. If we identify with the news we go mad. We get tossed and turned from one drama into the next, under the influence of the hallucinatory stories the crocodile keeps feeding us. You could say, unconsciously, we are drunk from believing our hallucinations without knowing it. Driving a car while under the influence of alcohol is unsafe. Living life under the influence of the crocodile is just as dangerous. We hurt ourselves and others through our unconscious actions without knowing it.

How can we wake up from our hallucination? The same way we wake up from a dream. We ask ourselves one simple question: Can I absolutely know that this is true? and hold whatever story is in our mind up to the light of this simple truth-finding inquiry.

But how do we remember to even ask the question? First, we need to to become conscious enough to inquire into our thinking. This is where our experience of ourselves helps. Untrue thoughts are unsettling—often at a very gross level, and sometimes more subtly, where we can only notice the untruth of a thought through a slightly unsettling energy in our bodies. To wake up from hallucination, we can simply scan our body for any tension, and ask that tension, "What are you wanting to tell me? What might you be afraid of?"

Tension comes in at least two flavors—cringing and clinging stress. Both tend to have the same root cause: believing that we are separate from love, not good enough, and unworthy. Our cringing crocodile is feeding us fight, flight, or freeze thinking: I need to attack to counter-attack, I need to run from attack, or I need to hide from attack. Attack thinking may show up as: I am better than you, I need to do this perfectly, I need to control you, I need to rescue you, I need to provide the answer, I am special, and I know everything. Running from thinking may include: I need to hold back what I think, I need to pretend, I need to please you, I need to avoid confrontation, I need to comply with the system, and I need to be flawless. And hiding thinking can sound like: I need to procrastinate, I am too overwhelmed to do anything, I am totally lost, I need to create drama so I don't need to face my own discomfort, and I secretly believe I know better than anyone and I am not going to tell them. Yes, our crocodile has quite a repertoire.

Different from cringing thinking, clinging thinking has us run toward a fantasy outcome, person, or feeling that we believe will make us whole. Our clinging crocodile has us believe that happiness is in the future and that our getting something that is not here already will get us there, whether it's a new possession, relationship, feeling, experience, or spiritual teaching. We believe this will finally get us the satisfaction we have been craving. Once the children are grown, or once we hit this benchmark, or once we understand this, or once we have lost this weight, or once we have gotten this settled, or once we own this, then.... Then we'll be content.

Whether it's cringing or clinging thinking, it doesn't matter. It won't hold up against the light of truth. All these stories try to convince us that we will finally feel at peace and loved once we have dealt with the danger and gotten ourselves to some imaginary outcome in the future. This is living like a beggar in our own palace. Giving time and attention to these untruths, we forget that we are already loved, love, and whole. That the peace we are racing to get is right here, right now.

As we wake up from our crocodilian clinging and cringing self-talk, we remember who we are—and we connect to the stillness underneath it all—presence, unconditional love, peace. Connected to our essence, we can look at our world and ask: How can I engage from the highest truth I see? Which may turn into: How can I love you and love myself today?

———

## Leadership Practice

*Make a brief inventory of your most frequent go-to crocodilian stories.*

*What kind of self-talk do you hear most often? Where do you feel this self-talk in your body? Who would you be without this self-talk?*

*Where in your life do you notice cringing thoughts? How does your body feel when these thoughts arise? Who would you be without these cringing thoughts?*

*Where in your life do you notice clinging thoughts? How does your body feel when these thoughts arise? Who would you be without these clinging thoughts?*

*Finally, say this mantra to yourself a few times throughout the day:*
*I let go of this habit of listening to untrue thoughts.*

# PRACTICE 43
## Inquiring from the Balcony of Being

G RAVITY, JUST LIKE presence, is always here. We can rely on it to help us plant our feet firmly on the ground and take our seat. Imagine a weightless existence. We have all seen images of astronauts floating around in space. There is something beautiful about that image, and also something slightly disorienting. Where is up or down without gravity? Where do we find stability?

Gravity helps us to stay grounded in our bodies, no matter what is going on around and within us. Even if our crocodiles are screaming havoc, we can always go back and feel our feet on the ground and our sits bones in our seat. Allowing gravity in, we develop gravitas. Both "gravity" and "gravitas" come from Latin *gravis*, which means "serious." Taking our seat, we don't play around; we are focused on the here and now.

We need groundedness to grow like the plant needs its roots firmly planted in the soil. What do we ground ourselves in beyond the physical experience of gravity? Allowing gravity in guides us into an energetic experience of groundedness. We become grounded in what lies beyond our thoughts and feelings, which are always fleeting, into something we can call presence, unconditional love, or even the sky, or the ground—symbolizing something that is always there, contains everything, and doesn't change in essence, no matter what the content is. It doesn't matter what clouds and weather patterns appear in the sky. The sky stays the sky. It also doesn't matter what we put on the ground. The ground stays the ground. Similarly, presence, awareness, doesn't change, no matter what thoughts and feelings we have.

Stepping into presence can feel like taking a step back from life, from the external stimuli and our thoughts and feelings. Since the pull of our thoughts and feelings is often strong, being present requires commitment. For a moment, we choose to become supremely disinterested in all our mental and emotional content, and allow ourselves to rest as the context—the context that never changes. It has been called the observer, and Ron Heifetz, the Harvard Kennedy School of Government professor, has coined it "the balcony." We go on the balcony of our experience and simply watch. We then take our seat on the balcony, resting in presence awareness.

Being on the balcony of our experience gives us perspective. Taking the step back to be on the balcony creates space between us and our experience, enough to allow us to dis-identify from the contents of our experience. From that place of the impartial observer, we simply watch *all* of the experiences. We inquire into truth. We see a thought appear in our experience. As opposed to having the next thought about it and creating a story, we go cold turkey. We stop. We ask: Can I absolutely know that this thought is true? We keep our seat on the balcony and just watch whatever appears. We don't even hang on to any insight. We stay supremely disinterested even in our insights, which are part of the *content* within the *context* of our unchanging awareness.

A friend of mine describes his experience of watching from the balcony as like watching a stage on which various parts of him show up as actors and speak his thoughts like lines in a play. Noticing who is speaking as each line is expressed often provides important clues about what unconscious motivations may be behind the thought. Over time, he describes it as coming to know the voices of a set of characters that represent different parts of him. Some bring crocodilian, fear-rooted thoughts and others the higher consciousness of the owl.

Does this mean we stay on the balcony observing and do nothing with any of our thoughts and feelings? No, not at all. Being on the balcony and patiently letting insight appear, in its time, we intuitively know when we hit on a deeper truth and when it's time to act. Until that time, we stay firmly rooted in the balcony. Truth insights often feel quiet and peaceful. A litmus test for truth can be: Is it peaceful, loving, and clear? Our bodies will tell us when we have found some truth. There is an inner quietude that comes with that. Half-truths feel restless, anxious, and unsettled. Feeling a half-truth, we simply stay on the balcony a little while longer. We let gravity in and take our seats more consciously. From that grounded place, with some distance between us and the contents of our experience, we ask—Is this true? Inquiry challenges all our beliefs, and I mean *all* our beliefs. With this deep humility—with "humility" coming from Latin *humus*, meaning "ground," we touch the ground of our being more and more deeply and start to see with the eyes of presence, as presence, where everything is seen as one and at the same time unique.

## Leadership Practice

*Allow gravity in to help you connect to your body more now. Let your body become deeply planted into the earth—let your feet touch the earth and rest in them, let your sits bones deeply rest in your chair. Notice how it feels to be deeply grounded, physically first and then, more broadly, energetically, in the here and now. Rest in that. Make a note of how it feels.*

*Then, from that grounded place, picture yourself on the balcony observing your inner landscape. Gently, patiently inquire into the thoughts and feelings of your experience. What do you notice about the energy of the thoughts and feelings? Can you know absolutely that what your thoughts and feelings are telling you is true?*

# PRACTICE 44
## Liberating Should-Thoughts

D RIVING ON A dam and causeway in the Netherlands, called the
*Afsluitdijk,* that links to northern provinces in the Netherlands and
has turned a sea arm—de *Zuiderzee*—into the *IJssel Lake,* protecting the
heart of the Netherlands from storm surges, I sometimes like to stop at
a little restaurant built on the dam. In that restaurant they have, besides
great apple pie, a series of pictures and journal clippings on the wall that
commemorate the building of the *Afsluitdijk* between 1927 and 1932 and
other historical events in Dutch history. Among them hangs a sun-faded
newspaper clipping discussing a national survey that polled people on
what for them was the most significant event of the twentieth century.
No, it's not the winning of the Eurocup in 1987, it's May 5, 1945,
Liberation Day—the day that the Netherlands was restored to freedom
from the occupation of the Nazis.

We love to be free. Free to be who we are, do what we like to do, go
where we like to go, be with whom we like to be with. We are wired for
freedom. We feel happiest when we are free, and often sad, anxious, and
frustrated when we are not. How do we attain freedom?

To become free, we need awareness of what keeps us hostage. It would
appear that true freedom comes from our external circumstances—and
certainly that is part of it. And yet, I have met and heard about people who
exude freedom while they are constrained by external circumstances, like
my Uncle Gerrit teaching me about love in the last few months of his life
while dying from cancer, and Nelson Mandela being a political activist
while in prison for twenty-seven years. How do we attain inner freedom
that is not dependent on external circumstances?

This is where we meet our crocodiles once again. Our crocodiles
conceptualize all day long about what should happen and compare it

144

to what is happening. Our fear-based crocodilian system is set up for survival, and control is one of its go-to strategies. This part of our nervous system tries to control everything all the time. And it does so, like a command-and-control management system, by measuring what is versus what should be, and having us exert endless effort to attain our imaginary safe state. Our crocodile is a micromanager who keeps score all day long.

Am I feeling the way I should feel? Am I getting what I think I should? Do I have in the bank what I should have? Am I productive the way I should be? Do people treat me the way they should? Am I kind the way I should be? Am I learning what I should? Am I making a difference the way I should? Am I having the intuition I should have? Am I enlightened the way I should be? And so on and so forth. Usually, several of our what-our-experience-should-be indicators are in the red. This is a clever way our crocodile has devised to keep us on the defensive, opposing reality in some way. The crocodile's nightmare is that we would dare to actually rest and relax into what is.

Who are we without all our defenses against reality? Who are we without all the mental conceptualizations about what should be? The crocodile rejects this reflection outright. It wants us to keep a healthy sense of anxiety. And it does so by keeping us busy with hallucinations about what should be.

According to the crocodile, without comparing what is to what should be, we never get what we want. Worse, we fall victim to all the dangers of being alive, chief among them our inevitable death. We try so hard not to die. I have not heard of anyone yet who has won this game.

Giving in to the should-be conceptualizations of the crocodile, we feel stressed, anxious, always somewhat worried. We live and lead from a prison, the walls of which are made of the conceptualizations of what should be. Who would we be, without any thought of what should be? What if we learned to accept, be with, and even love reality the way it is? What if we allowed ourselves to become one with reality? Then how would we live? How would we feel?

Try it out. Think of your should-belief *du jour*. Mine is "My partner should behave the way I want him to." How do I treat myself giving energy to this belief? Well, I feel anxious, thinking of strategies I can deploy to manipulate him to be and act in a way that fits my picture of the perfect partner. How do I treat him? I am being super nice to see if he will be swayed by my niceness to do what I want him to do. And how effective am I? This controlling thinking is consuming a significant part of my energy, which keeps me from taking care of the things I actually need to take care of.

Who would I be without this belief? If it were physically and mentally no longer possible for me to hold on to this belief that he should be any different from who he is? I would be free. I would be free to be me and see that he is free to be him. I would probably enjoy myself more, even be able to love myself and him more deeply. Dare I say I would connect to the inherent freedom of being that is not constrained by any mental conceptualizations?

Liberation Day in Dutch history was May 5, 1945. Liberation for me is one moment at a time. Every time I free myself from another should-thought, I loosen the grip of the crocodile's conceptualizations on me. This sometimes requires focus on my part, as I have lived under the occupation of many of these thoughts for years. Letting them go feels a bit like walking out of a prison that, after so many years of living there, has become my home.

"The truth will set you free." The question is: Do you want to be free, or do you prefer the comfort of your habitual hallucinations?

---

## Leadership Practice

*Think of a belief you have about what should be different— maybe a colleague who should act differently, or something that should happen differently from the way it is. Consider for a moment: Can you absolutely know that it is true that this should be different? Who would you be without this thought?*

*This doesn't mean that you become a doormat, or that you don't hold yourself and others accountable. It simply means that you are no longer identifying with a sense of reality that is untrue. You lose your worry and receive freedom and perspective in its place. You free yourself to be in this moment and, from the liberated point of view, see what is needed and do it.*

*Finally, say this mantra we introduced in an earlier practice to yourself a few times throughout the day:*
*I let go of this habit of listening to untrue thoughts.*

# PRACTICE 45
## Truth in Action

WE NATURALLY GRAVITATE to what is true. Applying the work of truth to ourselves as leaders, we come face to face with the fleetingness of all the identities we may try to hold on to for a while. Seven common ones, associated with Maslow's hierarchy of needs, are: I am the one who has material wealth, relationships, self-esteem, learning; I am the one who has made an impact, helps people see the bigger perspective, and is the wise and compassionate one. These are all ways, you could say, we could be of service that our crocodile turns into an identity we attach to. Free from crocodilian influence, we get to use this energy more constructively to create a stable home for ourselves and our family, nourish people around us with kindness, take care of ourselves by making something of our lives, enjoy learning and expanding our horizons, make an impact on the bigger world, learn to see the connection between everything, and grow in being and sharing wisdom and compassion. All of these are ways to express who we truly are. And as we express who we are, we get to know ourselves better. You could say we become more and more conscious of what we are truly made of, by putting what we are to work. A big part of that is sharing with others, as our essence magnetically seems to want to be shared—with everyone and everything around us.

Our fear-based crocodile hijacks our creative self-discovery journey by having us turn each temporary station, each way of expressing ourselves and being of service, into a fortress. Building a home for our family turns into us trying to create the perfect place to impress each other with. Caring for someone turns into defining ourselves by who we are with, and holding on to people and experiences far beyond their expiration date. Trying to make something of ourselves turns into a narcissistic pursuit at the expense of everything else; learning turns into the accumulation of importance; making a difference turns into becoming a savior; seeing the connection between things turns into becoming a know-it-all, and waking up to wisdom and compassion turns into becoming a teacher.

The good news is that truth won't have it. And since life is truth in action, it's really existence, life, that won't tolerate our staying in our fortresses for too long. Something in our external or internal environment will break to reveal to us that while we thought we were safe in our egoic enclosure, we were actually stuck believing ourselves to be a certain special separate someone, while we were the whole time only love, our essence, in action.

Heeding the call of truth from our essence, we let go of any identifications with any type of success as soon as it occurs. We let fortresses we unconsciously built over the years collapse as castles made of sky. That's really what they are. When we bring the light of truth, we realize that none of our identities are based in reality. They are based in crocodilian fantasies.

Without these identities, we get to lead with more lightness and dedication to what we are tasked with. Freed from the weight of having to look good, or come out looking better, and definitely not worse, we waste no more energy on self-aggrandizement. Instead, we can spend all that energy on taking care of what is right in front of us.

In this way, truth and love are two sides of the same coin. Being truthful, we let go of anything that is not us, which frees us up to be who we truly are—unconditional love—and bring that to every moment. We give love by bringing our analytical gifts, by connecting people, by listening deeply, by learning something new, by taking on a project that benefits others, by managing others in a caring way, by bringing intelligence to effectively leading towards a goal, or.... There are endless ways a leader can play the keyboard of love to care for people, the organization, and the task at hand.

From this vantage point, leadership is nothing but us learning to apply the essence we came in with—unconditional love—and getting to know it more deeply through our experiences. We get to know our true selves more deeply *through* the experience. Then, when we retire from our work, be it in the evening, or toward the latter parts of our lives, we simply smile, knowing a little bit more of what made us.

---

## Leadership Practice

*What is your go-to identity? How does it help you? How does it get in your way of being a truly effective leader?*


*Who would you be without this identity, and with complete dedication to the task at hand?*

# PRACTICE 46
## Truth Traveling

Truth moves through us and we move through truth. How do we access truth? There is always the foundation, the ground of our being, which we are coming to know as presence, unconditional love, peace, stillness. That feels true about us. Yet the truth of who we are cannot be captured; the more our perspective matures, the more aspects we discover about ourselves, like colors in a rainbow. We may discover that our kindness is not only soft, it also has firmness to it. We may see that our wisdom is not only vast, it's also very precise and meticulous. We may find that our drive is not only forward, it's also inward. In our journey of self-discovery we're never done; we are always standing on the edge of new revelation.

Our crocodiles don't like being on the edge at all. They would rather force us into one hallucinatory belief system about what reality is and be done with it. That's safe and comfortable. Driven by our crocodilian drive for control, we lose our capacity to be patient and let the truth about ourselves and the situation we are in emerge. From a growth perspective, every situation offers some kind of window into who we truly are and how to be of service from that place. From a crocodile's vantage point, every situation is about us becoming safer, and thus we retreat, with everything life offers, more deeply into the fortress of our false beliefs. From the crocodile's perspective, everything is either a confirmation of our beliefs or an attack on it. Being confirmed in what we believe, we become more self-righteous. Feeling attacked, we counterattack by making the other, or even ourselves, wrong, retreating into a popular crocodilian fortress—the one of constant judgment.

Freeing ourselves from crocodilian rigidity, we see truth as something to be explored. We see that truth moves through us and we move through it as well. We open to truth in space and time. We open to truth in space by allowing ourselves to take a different vantage point on the challenge we are facing. We might choose to hang out in the shoes of another party who is involved in the challenge at hand and ask, How would they experience the situation? What would they really yearn for? What might their crocodile be afraid of? We travel to them in our minds and hearts and see the situation from their perspective for a while, before going home again to our own perspective. Then we take a balcony view, and see—What if all of us were right? Then what becomes true about this situation? How would we approach it then?

By traveling to other perspectives, we develop a systems view that integrates different ways of seeing and softens the separation that our crocodile keeps fighting for. We become milder as we start to see the situation from many points of view at the same time. Traveling through space, we meet different aspects of ourselves, as our perspective deepens with compassion for the other and broadens with insight from the other.

Our crocodiles find this exercise a colossal waste of time. They would rather stay home in the well-defended perspective they know so well. They want to have answers now! When we open the heart to a situation it loses its immediacy and turns from an event into a road on which we travel. We become more able to be patient and let the dust settle. We don't rush. We simply keep walking, one breath at a time, opening our hearts to the situation a little bit more and allowing time to heal any misperceptions in us. Over time, and yet always in the here and now, we stumble into new insights. We don't force them. They simply come to us, like sunrays touching our face.

The word *insight* comes down through Middle English and implies the idea of "inner sight." Seeing into the truth doesn't happen on a schedule. We can't force insight, just as we can't force our breathing and digestion. It simply happens.

What we can do is to create the conditions where having insight becomes easier. We can facilitate our breathing, by taking a few deep conscious breaths into the belly and allowing any tension in our bodies to leave. We can help our digestion by being mindful about our eating and movement habits. We can make ourselves more ready to receive insights, to gain inner vision, by opening the eyes of our heart. With the eyes of the heart, we can observe without pushing for an answer. With the eyes of the heart, we are naturally drawn to others' perspectives and to learning more about them. With the eyes of the heart, we rest with a soft gaze on anything that crosses our path.

With the eyes of the heart, we see we are always on a journey. We see that we are always evolving. With the eyes of the heart we learn to appreciate, even enjoy, the journey to ever more truth.

---

## Leadership Practice

*Look around where you are. Take the perspective of different things in your space. How would the doorknob see you? How would the chair see you? What about the ground? Or the ceiling?*

*What are you learning as you patiently take these different perspectives in? How does looking at yourself from these different perspectives change the way your body feels in this moment?*

# PRACTICE 47
## The Be-Here-Now Focus Button

WHEN WE GIVE ourselves to this moment, this moment gives to us. I just discovered the "focus" button in the word processing program on my computer. When I press it, all the tools and icons of other programs disappear—even the clock is no longer here. I am left with just a blank screen and my document. This is actually quite confronting. I notice how much of my mind is used to having distraction readily available—of a new email coming in, a text message from someone, or even the soothing sense of knowing what time it is. My mind likes to distract itself.

Our crocodile doesn't try to distract us only with such seemingly benign diversions. It also has us in constant evaluation mode: How did I do? What will happen next? Regret about the past and worry about the future are some of its favorite pastimes. Pastime is a great word for it. We literally pass up the time and give our time and attention away to what is not even here. We waste our time and attention on hallucinations—our mental projections of the past and the future. In the meantime, reality is simply here. It is always here, whether we notice it or not.

This is why the practice of being present in the here and now is so potent. Yes, it's a practice that takes some time to cultivate, as we are not used to being in the present moment. We are used to mentally being anywhere but the present moment. We are so busy evaluating everything that we forget to be here.

Being here, right now, can feel a bit like detox. But what about this email? Or what about my being on time? Or what about this unresolved issue? Our crocodile, being focused on our survival, is not interested in our being fully here now. That would be way too dangerous. Who knows what might happen if we weren't ready to defend our past or protect our future?

Well, let's try it out. Let's be here now. Let's be completely dedicated to this moment. Let all thoughts and feelings, which try to draw us back into a story about the past and the future, or even a story about this moment, go. Let it all go. And be totally here.

You may find that you meet an aliveness inside of yourself. A sense of space. Maybe a feeling of warmth and wonder. Interestingly, you may find yourself feeling clear. An insight about something may even drop in. Don't try to grasp it. It will be here when you need it.

Being present in the here and now, we connect with reality as it is, not as we think it should be. We directly look beyond our thoughts and feelings into what this moment is truly about. By being present, we part the walls of perception and peek into the reality of this moment.

This is a skill we can practice. Over time, being present can become something that is more second nature to us. Imagine what will become possible for you when you are no longer in your mind, but connect directly with reality as it is. How alive would you feel? How would you connect differently with others? What would happen with your creativity and sense of flow?

I notice this in coaching sessions. Sometimes my crocodile wants to take over, thinking I am too tired, busy, or stressed to truly surrender to this moment. As a crocodilian coach, I am not here—only my mental conceptualizations about reality are here. The coachee will feel this. They won't feel seen. When I notice that my crocodile is trying to do the coaching for me, I have learned to breathe deeply, pause, and let go of all my thoughts and feelings for a moment. This doesn't mean that they will be gone, it only means that I will have loosened my grip on them, no longer giving them my time and attention. Instead I focus on this moment, with the coachee and me in it. Invariably, the wisdom of the moment will become apparent. As I listen to it, the conversation moves as if by itself. We are back in flow.

Deeply connecting to this moment helps us tap into our essence beyond the stories of our minds. Our stories are mostly reruns of old themes. The wisdom of the present moment is always fresh.

Giving ourselves to the present moment, we discover its aliveness; we become it. We unite with the whole of life and start playing our part in it, effortlessly, as the violin player in the orchestra who, deeply attuned to the whole body of the sound, intuitively knows how and when to play. Sometimes I close my eyes to access the present moment. It's my way to press my "focus" button. I take a deep breath and simply allow myself to be here.

Being in the present moment frees us from mental chatter. Being here now, we meet reality.

---

## Leadership Practice

*Allow yourself to breathe deeply into your belly three times. Now allow your attention to rest in this moment. Notice any thoughts and feelings as clouds in the sky. Let them pass through you, and come back to this present moment. Allow yourself to become even more present.*

*What is your experience being here now?*

# PRACTICE 48
## Unobscured Mind

THE MORE WE are grounded in reality—the more we see clearly—the wiser, more compassionate, and effective we'll be as leaders and human beings. In the Buddhist Heart Sutra, one of my favorite lines reads: "Since there is no obscuration of mind, there is no fear." The crocodile pulls the wool over our eyes. The crocodile literally obscures our mind with fear. With the eyes of the crocodile we don't see reality as it is, we see a distorted version of it. We see what we fear rather than seeing the truth of reality.

Seeing reality without our mental conceptualizations about it, we see things as *they* are, not as *we* are. We see ourselves and others as we truly are, not as our crocodile makes us out to be. A core belief of the crocodile is that we are separate ego identities stacked up against each other in an endless struggle for coming out on top. Our crocodile wants to make sure we don't lose and sees danger lurking in every moment. From our crocodile's point of view, life is heavy and only becomes heavier over time. We may start with a small fear thought, like "They may not like me," and move to a bigger one—"I should comply to be the way they want me to," to "I should keep up this perfect pleasing image that I have constructed over the years," to "I am getting exhausted keeping this up, and I am pissed off that others make me do this," to "I am blaming them for all difficulties in my life," to "I should do something to change them so I can feel better about myself," to "I need to get others to change so I have a higher chance of winning," to starting an outright fight. A tiny fear thought can have huge consequences. Unchecked, it can grow into a huge wilderness that dominates our lives and hurts others.

This doesn't mean that reality doesn't include danger. It certainly does. Even seen with the eyes of truth, fire is still hot, ice is still cold, and if we walk into an abyss we likely still die. It's just that seeing truthfully, we don't give energy to any of our stories about life. We simply look directly in the face of what is here. And we use discernment to decide what we need to do now, just like a river knows which way to turn around a rock. The river doesn't know until it reaches the rock which way to turn. It simply turns as it meets the rock. Living in the moment, living and leading from presence, we have clear discernment about what is, rather than believing our crocodilian projections.

Freeing ourselves from crocodilian projections takes concentration. Why? Because most of us carry a lot of crocodilian stories around that we have been replaying from very early on in our lives. Since childhood, we have been adding more and more stories, forming thicker and thicker layers of fearful stories that obscure our truthful seeing. I believe that if we are lucky, our crocodilian stories become so intolerable at some point that we say: Enough! I can't do this anymore. Something in us breaks and reality has a chance to peek through. This happens with the addict who reaches the end of his rope, seeing that the substance actually destroys rather than saves him. This happens with teams who run up against their own limiting mindsets and behaviors as they become ineffective in reaching their goals. This happens with the leader who gets more responsibility and comes face to face with his own stories—for example, about having to be the Perfect One, the Rescuer, or the Martyr and realizes he can't operate anymore in this way to be effective.

Of course, we don't have to wait for life to break our cocoon of crocodilian hallucination. We can decide to put our time and attention to what's most important to us. If that is being truthful, living and leading from an unobscured place, we'll learn to approach every moment from that self-liberating vantage point. We learn to tame our crocodiles, moment to moment, and let them go. We learn to let go of our hallucinations about what reality is and we start to live from reality as it is.

The more we see clearly what is, the less fearful we become. We experience fear as the opposite of truth. That is good news. When we are fearful, we know we are not truthful. We are filled with hallucinations and are believing them to be reality. When we are truthful, we are empty of stories and full of this moment. Experiencing fear simply becomes an invitation to inquire for truth: Is this fear I have true? Who would I be without it? Then how would I approach this moment?

---

## Leadership Practice

*What do you fear? What is the story your crocodile wants you to believe?*


*Who would you be without this fear? What is a more truthful perspective of what is actually happening? How can you respond differently, from an unobscured perspective?*

## PRACTICE 49
### Connecting to True Perspective

THE MORE WE give ourselves to truth, the more it gives itself to us. Giving ourselves to truth can feel like taking an internal shower. We clean ourselves from layers of untruth—false beliefs we learned somewhere along the way. Giving ourselves to truth, we feel supported by it. We are joining the harmony of existence and we start to resonate with it. We relax; our breathing becomes deeper and flows more naturally. We become one with existence.

Giving ourselves to truth is empowering. Giving into untruth is disempowering. In truth, we don't second-guess ourselves. We are simply here. I have noticed this in conflicts I have been in. The more I don't listen to myself, my deeper truth, the more unstable I feel. My mind starts racing, trying to keep up with everyone else's opinions and crocodiles. Actually, our crocodiles are working against each other, hoping that the smartest, wisest, loudest, most dramatic, or most manipulative one will walk away with the grand prize—being right and winning the others over to our side.

Pausing, breathing deeply, and asking myself quietly, "What is true here?" helps me to come back to reality and leave the crocodilian hallucinatory racetrack. I start to take it easy and things become simpler. I relax into the here and now, into the truth that unites us all—presence, unconditional love. From that place, I see things from their true perspective, from the perspective of presence, unconditional love. The first thing I notice is that things that seemed a huge deal only a few minutes ago are actually much ado about nothing. I can feel the oxygen come back into my perception. With that oxygenated view, things look more vibrant, more alive, and more benign to me. I don't see things as threatening anymore. I start to discern what is actually called for versus what my and others' crocodilian ideas are.

As the crocodilian dust settles, truth comes into view. The deeper truth about the situation becomes more palpable. I almost touch it. I know what to do. Often this means doing absolutely nothing, to simply absorb, and be still. Often the truth is that I have been very confused. That my crocodiles have made me think and feel I was in some sort of crisis I should resolve now. Relaxing, taming my crocodilian thinking, I start to sense the subtleties in the situation at hand.

Sometimes this leads me to big, bold action. For example, grounded in truth—and yes, this doesn't always come slowly; it can come like a lightning bolt revelation—I decide to take a stand for something, without taking a stand against others. I take a stand for truth, for acceptance, for freedom, and leave unhealthy relationships. I discontinue projects, seeing that our motivation is fear-based, nothing to do with my highest truth.

Bold action based in truth actually doesn't feel bold at all. It feels natural and clear, like what is supposed to happen. Being grounded in truth, we connect with the power that comes with it. Gandhi's movement was called *satyagraha*, which also means "truth force." When we connect to the truth within us, we connect with a power far greater than our fickle crocodilian mind can muster. We connect with a truth that has no real opposition. It simply is.

Being committed to truth requires deep humility. We can easily mistake being truthful for having *the* truth. Being truthful is being dedicated to the ongoing inquiry of what is true, without claiming any of it for ourselves. In a conflict, it's not your opinion versus mine; it's what is true for all of us that will resolve the conflict. What is really true here? we may ask. What do you really care about that is even more important than the position you have taken? How is what you care about and what I care about the same? How can we take care of what we both care about in the best possible way?

Our crocodiles hide behind brittle defenses. They try to have us justify our positions. Our owl simply sighs and says: I don't know yet. I don't know yet and I am going to open myself to find out. When we are ready for truth, we want to touch the ground, the foundation that unites us all. What is really true here? What is true for you? What is true for them? What is true for all of us? How can we see and act from an integrated view that blends these multiple perspectives?

With this truth, we connect to a power greater than ourselves that doesn't give us power *over* others and things, but rather power *to* act on truth. It connects us to the power of truth and love to do what is needed, without looking back, completely in this moment, in the here and now. Truth power brings us together, as it comes from a perspective that unites rather than divides, that is eternal rather than temporary, and that is based in unconditional love rather than our fear-based conditioning.

## Leadership Practice

*Reflect on a dilemma you are facing. Take note of what your crocodile wants you to worry about and do about it.*

*Now allow yourself to slow down and take a few slow, conscious breaths into the belly. Allow yourself to drop all your stories about the situation. What is true for you? What may be true for other stakeholders involved? What is a truth that unites all of you?*

*When you feel settled, grounded in this truth, how can you act on this truth?*

# PRACTICE 50
## Living Our Highest Truth

Having gotten a taste of truth is both a blessing and a curse. It blesses us with the power, the peace, the joy, and the love that come online when we are in it. Truth blesses us also with choice. We can choose to listen to our truth or not. This is where the curse lies. Knowing truth, we can no longer not know it. Something deep inside of us always remembers truth. Acting out of integrity with our truth feels much more painful once we know our truth.

Once I know what it's like to be honest, I feel much more vividly what dishonesty feels like. Once I know what it's like to truly see the other for who they are, it becomes that much more impossible to judge them. Once I sense what pace of work is truly in harmony with myself, it becomes that much more impossible to work harder or less hard than my truth calls from me. Truth is a demanding father and a nourishing mother. Truth demands our integrity and gives us the power to act on it.

Choosing truth can feel like stepping into a tug-of-war. Dare I be so honest that people may leave me? Dare I be so accepting that I can no longer protect myself with judgment? Dare I become so generous that I may not get what I think I want? Dare I become so firmly grounded in my purpose that I no longer give in to distractions? On the one hand, I want to be truthful; on the other hand, I would like to keep my life as comfortable as it seems to be right now.

Our crocodiles, hell bent on our ego's survival, will do everything in their power to keep us asleep. Being truthful equals losing the safety strategies they have devised so cleverly over all these years. "Yes, but maybe you don't need to be truthful today, you could just wait till you feel better," suggests one crocodile. Another one adds: "Yes, and what will truth get you? You have worked so hard to build up your sense of self!

Do you want to lose all of that?!" A very sly one says: "Yes, and you don't know your truth anyway. You are far too inexperienced to stand in your truth. You should know your place. And that is back in the comfort of your habitual thinking and acting."

Which way do we go? Do we take the path of truth or the path of habit? The path of habit—oh, well, yes; we know that one, by definition. The path of truth is an open path. We don't know where it will lead us. The path of habit promises safety and certain outcomes. The path of truth promises nothing, only gives us a sense of being in integrity with our truth, come what may. How do we walk this path?

One step at a time. Every step of the way we can embody our highest truth. A life path of truth consists of millions of steps taken one at a time. I read online that "the average person (moderately active) takes around 7,500 steps per day. If this was maintained daily through the age of eighty, you will have walked about 216,262,500 steps throughout your life." Every step of these millions of steps, we have a choice. Do I take a step coming from truth, or do I take a step driven by crocodilian hallucination? I can feel the difference in my walking. Walking in truth, every step has a tiny quality of exhilaration about it. It's fulfilling to know that I lived my highest truth in this moment. Giving into untruth, I will feel unease.

Remember the sly crocodile saying, "Yes, but you don't know your truth anyway?" This is a tricky one. We may find ourselves in many situations where we indeed feel confused, rattled, unsure of what to think, say, or do. In these moments, we can come back to our deeper selves, simply by taking a few deep conscious breaths and connecting to the space beyond our thoughts and feelings, the sky in us, unconditional love, presence. Resting in that sense of presence, we let our crocodiles calm down and let our quiet sense of true self come to the foreground. We find in ourselves the wherewithal to go stand in our own shoes and take the next step, informed by who we truly are.

It's a journey of truth, not a destination. It's about progress, not perfection. We act from the highest truth we have realized and trust that the next wise step will reveal itself in the next present moment. Wisdom happens moment to moment. It is something that comes to us. It's a paradox. While we don't hold on to any of the wisdom as ours, we do take a firm stand for what we see now. In that way, we get to know our truth more deeply as we act from it. Being honest, we learn about honesty. Being kind, we learn about kindness. Being firm, we learn about firmness; and being open, we learn about openness.

It's a choice we have moment to moment. Do I take the next step in the adventure of truth? Or do I go back to sleep and keep copying and pasting my past experiences onto this moment?

## Leadership Practice

*Jot down a few words about your highest truth. What do you sense your life is about? What is the most important thing for you? What would happen if you took the next step in your life based on your current sense of your highest truth?*

# PART 6

## Walking and Working with Others

## PRACTICE 51
### Keeping My Crocodiles Out of the Conversation

WHAT DO YOU really want for and from your relationships? Our crocodile is clear. They are for ME! They are here to help me feel safe and in control.

Our crocodiles will skillfully use relationships to get what they want. Conversations turn into grab-fests for our ego. Let's take a look at seven intentions a crocodile may walk into a conversation with. Each intention is there to help our scared little crocodile take care of one of his core fears:

1. *Fear of Scarcity:* Under the influence of the fear of scarcity, I use every conversation to help further my financial objectives. What will be the ROI on this conversation? our crocodile asks. How do I get better off by talking to you? This crocodile will *prioritize money over being truthful*, respectful, and other aspects of being in integrity with myself.

2. *Fear of Abandonment:* Driven by this fear, I play nice, or not nice at all. I try to keep my friends close and judge people who are different from me and who don't agree with me. I use conversations to cement my cliques, at the expense of being authentic and empathic. All of this to help keep my crocodilian support network intact. *The tribe trumps the truth* is this crocodile's motto.

3. *Fear of Failure:* Because I should never fail, I go into conversations with ready-made conclusions and decisions. I do not let people into the messiness of my feelings, assumptions, and interpretations—the kitchen of my creative process. I only meet people in the executive dining room where the food of my

conclusions is ready to be plated. I do not get my fingers dirty exchanging feelings and initial thinking with others. It would be terrible if others saw that I don't have it all figured out, and, yes, that I make mistakes. Imagine that! *Say it perfectly or don't say it at all*, thinks this crocodile.

4.  *Fear of Uncertainty:* The crocodile is allergic to uncertainty. It sees what could happen as *only* negative, so it pretends uncertainty doesn't exist. Speaking with others, I state my opinions as facts, and make others wrong for not agreeing with me. Really, I believe they are stupid, they are not getting it. Conversations are transactions for which I write the terms. I know what the outcome should be and I manipulate people by dominating them with strong opinions and rigid meeting agendas. Also, being overly dramatic is a great strategy to get the outcome I want, believes this crocodile. *Let me tell you how it is*, shouts this crocodile with a hermetically closed heart.

5.  *Fear of Hurt:* Yes, people not liking what I say is part and parcel of conversations—that is, if I dare to have real conversations, which my crocodile is not interested in at all. The crocodile is terrified of any kind of pain. To make sure people will like me, or really have no other choice but to like me, I inflate my sense of importance, trying to rescue others, or being the hero that saves the day—always knowing just what the right answer is to everything. *Leave it to me*, is the self-congratulatory stance of this crocodile.

6.  *Fear of Complexity:* People may say things that disturb my neat sense of order in the world. Our crocodile likes to solve problems now, immediately, and has no capacity to deal in ambiguity and complexity, as that, according to the crocodile, will only get me into trouble. Being a naysayer, doomsday prophet, or sage are wonderful postures for the crocodile, to keep its fantasy of *I understand everything* intact.

7.  *Fear of Losing Identity:* Going into a conversation not knowing how I will be perceived, I introduce myself as a special so-and-so, with such-and-such credentials, so I don't have to do the hard work of being fully in the moment and letting what needs to be said come naturally. Instead I use every conversation to strengthen my self-image, letting people subtly, or not so subtly, know who I am. I put myself on a pedestal— or do the opposite, letting people know I have nothing to contribute. Being a martyr is another great way to separate myself from the rest of the riffraff in the conversation. This crocodile thinks that *every conversation is about me, about who else would it be?*

Conversations are such great food for the crocodile. Unfortunately, when we let the crocodile eat up our conversations, all of us, including ourselves, are left feeling hungry, as opposed to nourished. The crocodiles squander the beauty of human exchange, which has so much potential. It can be a place of mutual support, connection, purposeful action, discovery, extending care, integration, and self-recognition, when we don't give in to any one of the crocodilian claims on this precious space.

## Leadership Practice

*Reflect on a conversation you are about to have. Which of the following crocodiles, if any, may try to distract you from bringing your true self to the conversation? How would you approach the conversation differently, free from this crocodile?*

1.  *Fear of Scarcity: I prioritize money over being truthful*

2.  *Fear of Abandonment: My tribe trumps the truth*

3.  *Fear of Failure: I need to say it perfectly or not say it at all*

4.  *Fear of Uncertainty: Let me tell you how it is*

5.  *Fear of Hurt: Leave it to me*

6.  *Fear of Complexity: I understand everything*

7.  *Fear of Losing Identity: It's all about me, who else would it be about?*

# PRACTICE 52
## Seven Owl Intentions for Conversation

T<small>HINK OF THE</small> best conversations you have ever had. Chances are you felt alive, maybe taller on the inside, deeply connected with the other person, and creative. The word *conversation* comes from Latin *conversari*, meaning to "turn together" or "change together." In a great conversation, all parties change a bit—maybe because we feel heard—leave with a new insight, feel more deeply connected with another person, or see new possibilities to address a situation that we didn't see before.

Our crocodile believes that conversations happen *to* us. We may be on guard: What will the other person say? Will I be able to handle that? How do I keep control of the conversation? How do I get what I want? For the crocodile, conversations are hard work that it wants to be done and over with quick.

From our higher owl consciousness, we can see conversations as invitations to learn, to be ourselves, to be open to one another, and to discover and create something together. It's something we look forward to. While we can't make a conversation go our way—sorry, crocodile, I know that's what you want—we are part of the conversation. We focus on the part that is within our control—that is how we show up, the energy we bring to the conversation. What is our unconditional intention? Unconditional, meaning that it doesn't depend on how the conversation "goes" and how the other responds.

Reflecting on this question itself can give us energy. Reflection by itself puts us in a state of mind that is more aligned with our true essence. How can I bring presence, unconditional love, peace into this conversation? How can I share my full self and respect their full selves?

Having a few pointers can be helpful to shape our intention. In the Eastern wisdom traditions, they conceived of a system called the chakras, which maps our energy system, how our centers of energy and intelligence are organized in the body. This system distinguishes seven chakras that each correspond to an area in our body. You'll notice below that Maslow's hierarchy of needs reflects these energy centers. Going into conversation, we can take a moment and check in with each of these energy centers to make sure they are turned on. It's like combing our hair and brushing our teeth. We want to show up clean. We ensure that our crocodiles are not hijacking any of these energy centers for their own ego-preservation goals.

Let's check in with each of the seven energy centers in our body now, and explore the highest intentions we can set for any conversation, for each of them. I have written in *italics* a word we can use to remind ourselves of the energy of the chakra, followed by where the energy center is in our bodies and how we can interact from this chakra.

1.  *Samurai:* Sacrum and sits bones. Grounded in our seat, we intend to stay rooted in our own energy, to be resourceful by being fully present in this moment on the earth, to stay true to the facts and to stay out of stories.

2.  *Uniting:* Lower belly. We allow ourselves to feel our feelings, without being slaves to them. We open fully to where the other is now, to their feelings and perspective. We dare, for a moment, to take their seat and see the situation from their perspective. We allow ourselves to become empathetic without losing ourselves in the other. We keep walking in our own two shoes being authentic, and tune in to where the other may be going.

3.  *Centered in Purpose:* Solar plexus. We remind ourselves what we stand for, without standing against others. We reflect on our goal, and assert it freely, without trying to overpower the other. We stay strongly focused on where we are going and why.

4.  *Curious:* Heart, chest area. We open our heart to this present moment, including all our feelings, our thoughts, and what we sense from the other person. We stay curious and open. We keep a question mark on our heart. We share what is true for us with vulnerability. We open our heart even a bit more to what is and let the magic of the conversation take care of itself.

5. *Extending Contribution:* Throat. We say what we need to say, unapologetically. We speak our truth, as *our truth*. We keep asking ourselves: What is the highest truth I see now? How can I speak from this place? We enjoy sharing who we are and what we see. We share what we say as a gift, free from attachment to whether the receiver likes it or not.

6. *Sensing:* Area between the eyebrows. We are fully engaged in the conversation and at the same time quietly feel into what is happening from our balcony as the observer. We allow ourselves to take multiple perspectives, and reflect on: What is really true here? What if all of us were right? Then how would I see this? We listen to our intuition to guide us when to speak, when to listen, and what words to use.

7. *Simple:* Top of the head. We realize that we are an infinitesimally small part of the universe and of time. We approach this moment with great humility. We are grateful we get to be part of it and contribute our piece. At the same time, we sense the vastness that we are, and that we are part of. We allow that vastness to come through us. We may have a sense of being held, being empowered, and being spoken through in the conversation.

Reflect on any of these seven owl intentions for conversation. Check in how it feels to connect with these words from the place of the body that they are written for. Don't worry about doing it right. These words are just pointers to help you bring your highest self to the conversation.

## Leadership Practice

*Think of a challenging conversation you need to have. What is the highest intention you can have for this conversation? Which of the seven owl intentions would be most helpful for you to focus on? What would happen if you allowed a bit more of that intention to flow into the conversation? Then, what would become possible?*

## PRACTICE 53
### Interim and Authentic Truth Speaking

Words only approximate reality. We call a tree a tree, while it's really something that goes beyond description. The same can be said about every word we ever speak or think. They are only conceptualizations of reality. Then why even bother? Why try to speak with each other? And how can we speak skillfully?

Our thinking is a helpful pointer to what is true. It helps us navigate our world. Without thoughts, we would relate very differently to our world and we'd miss out on all the beauty human thought can create. Think of any of the magnificent buildings you have been in, or a beautiful highway you have driven on, or an uplifting piece of music that has touched you. Our thoughts help us create beauty that uplifts us. Speaking our thoughts helps us to relate to another and create beauty together—speaking with each other, we share perspectives, learn from each other, appreciate, connect, make requests and promises, even dream, plan, and coordinate, so that our thoughts become physical reality.

How do we speak well? A helpful place to start is to observe who is talking. Is it my fearful crocodilian conditioning, or my wise owl? Am I speaking from my ego persona or from the infinite, limitless place that unites us all? Letting our crocodile take over, we use our speech to help us get ahead in the world, to solidify our sense of self: the Good One, the Bad One, the Special One, the Nice One, the Avoidant One etc. From my owl, from presence, awareness, I am magnetically drawn to what is true. I want to know what is true—it's part of my nature. I sense it's part of all our natures. Something in us cringes when we speak or hear an untruth. And something else in us celebrates when we share truth.

Speaking truthfully is an owl intention. And it's a tall order. How do we speak truth? There are so many layers of semi-truth in my consciousness that cloud what is true. Yet, when I wait long enough, sometimes by taking some distance from a particular issue, I gain perspective and discover more truth, even though I can never completely think and say the whole truth, as my words never reach that far into reality. That doesn't mean I don't try. It's like trying to say to someone you really love, that you love them, knowing full well that you never transmit the truth of your feelings through words alone.

Speaking truth requires patience and self-reflection. Is what I am saying true? Or is it my crocodile trying to manipulate its way to some sense of pseudo-certainty? We know we have arrived at a deeper truth, because it feels more stable. It doesn't need arguing. It's simply here. All we needed to do was to simply stop and see. What is really true here? We call this our *Authentic Truth*. We haven't arrived at this deeper truth, when we haven't found a sense of peace with it yet. We're still debating inside of ourselves.

Sometimes it's helpful to share our inner debate with others. After we have scrubbed our thinking from the crocodilian aggressive and defensive stuff a bit, we share what we are thinking now without judging, blaming, putting down, making special, forcing things, or attaching to any particular outcome. We don't need to let the crocodilian thinking soil our connection with others. It's not their job to clean up our thinking. It is ours. Once we have scrubbed our thinking from its crocodiles, we are more able to see what is true and share that with others, even if we haven't quite landed yet on that restful, peaceful thought that's closer to the truth. We can call this in-between place our *Interim Truth*. I find that sharing my Interim Truth with others frees me from my self-imposed yoke that I need to have it all figured out. Putting my Interim Truth next to someone else's Interim Truth gives both of us a stronger perspective on the truth that underlies our conversation. I might say: "Hey, I am still pondering this and what I am thinking now is... What is your perspective?"

Truth speaking may come with a sense of humility and lightness, because we realize that our words are only fingers pointing to the moon, not the moon itself. It can also have a quality of charisma and gravitas to it. The word *charisma* comes from the Greek word *kharis*, meaning "favor" or "grace." Our speaking becomes charismatic as we grace each other through words that are intended to be truthful. Then our speaking becomes a gift, an act of love. And speaking our truth may help others find theirs.

Speaking truth can be gentle and firm at the same time. Sometimes we need to use words to say things others may not like, such as holding someone accountable or making a challenging request to them. If we can do so with deep care for the other and zero judgment, we likely are relating from a more truthful place. Then an extreme speech action, like firing someone, can feel like an act of love, because it is. We are speaking truth as we see it, inviting the other to see more truth as well.

Yet even when we are authentic and caring, the other may still get triggered and their crocodile may drive their immediate reaction to us. For us, that's a call to hold space and patiently listen, without getting enmeshed in their reactivity. We may say "Thank you for sharing," and move on.

We can never claim to have the full truth, because we don't. Reality is infinite and our minds are not. We can only approximate reality. This also means that we sometimes will not see eye to eye on some things. The crocodile doesn't like this. It forces premature consensus. The owl, on the other hand, simply rests and observes to let a truer perspective come to the foreground.

Truth is a journey. Every moment, we get a chance to learn more about the truth of who we really are and what our external circumstances are about. Are you interested to find out more truth today?

## Leadership Practice

*Think about a challenge where you don't quite know what to do yet. Take a moment to step back from it. What is your Interim Truth about it? What if you shared this Interim Truth with someone else involved in the situation and see what you can discover together?*

*What if you shared your Interim Truth even if it might trigger a crocodilian reaction in the other? What if you can hold a space of non-judgment and listen deeply to their responses as a way to find a path forward to an even deeper Interim Truth?*

## PRACTICE 54
## Deep Detached Listening

WHAT DOES IT feel like to be deeply listened to? Maybe you sense relief, connection with the other, possibly a sense of greater freedom and peace now that you have been able to get something off your chest. Have you noticed that really being listened to doesn't require much of a response from the other? The other being present with us seems to be all that's required to really feel listened to.

Our crocodile complicates our listening, like it complicates everything else, as it believes everything it hears needs a reaction, to make sure it's ok. Is it true that we need to respond to what we hear? Who would you be without this belief? How much more deeply, and more freely, would you be able to listen to another if you didn't have to respond? You could observe what is being said as if in meditation, observing the thoughts and feelings without attaching to any of them, simply letting them go as they come along. This may seem like a callous way to listen. Wasn't I supposed to show good listening by repeating back what they said, or at least respond to it? I know I learned that somewhere...

We can listen by being attached to our agenda of having to respond to everything, or we can listen with detachment. What they say is not about us. The other person is trying to say something that is important to them. We can listen, observe, and feel what is being said in between the words in their energy, tone of voice, rhythm, and body language. What is the person really saying? What is true for them? What is their "Authentic Truth" about? Grounded in detached listening, and being present, we may hear intuition nudge us to ask a question to go deeper. Or maybe not. For sure, our crocodile has tons of questions, because everything that is being said is really about us and we need to make sure we are safe.

Detached listening is deep listening. What would it be like to truly be with another, without having to get anything from them? This may seem like an anathema in our world that is so focused on transactions. *I give you this so you will give me that. I will listen to you, so you will give me the deal, your approval, etc.*, goes our self-talk. What would it be like to suspend our agendas for a moment and truly listen to another?

This doesn't mean we become inactive. On the contrary. We listen deeply, and, if needed, hone in on what we sense needs to be explored more deeply. From the shared clarity that emerges, we may start to exchange ideas about what, if anything, we need to do about what we just learned. Be mindful, though. Our crocodile is addicted to activity as a way to control things. The crocodile never rests and doesn't want us to either. Ask yourself, after having listened deeply to another: Is there really something for me to do here, or is it my crocodile trying to satisfy its restlessness?

Deep listening doesn't mean that we don't care about or are indifferent to the other person. Deep listening is an act of love. We are here, representing our essence, presence, unconditional love, simply being here. This may seem like nothing. And yet it can be everything. Sometimes just helping the other person verbalize their thoughts by being there with them helps them to gain clarity. And often their clarity sparks greater clarity in ourselves.

Listening deeply, we dissolve the boundaries between you and me, reflecting together on what may be true about us. That is energizing. It nourishes. It's creative. When two become one in presence, ideas start flowing, there is joy, a shared strength comes online, and we feel deeply alive, often taller on the inside. Deep listening helps us connect with our shared essence. Deep listening helps us feel at home with each other and ourselves.

Practice deep listening right now as you read these pages. Listen deeply to yourself. Practice detached listening and notice what you hear from the depth of your being. As a deep listener, you are simply here, without needing to do something. If there is an action that needs to happen, you will know when it's time.

## Leadership Practice

*Listening deeply to someone this week, practice detachment. Notice what happens when you allow yourself to be with the other person, without needing to do anything. What new possibilities for being and doing emerge from this quality of interaction?*

# PRACTICE 55
## The Nourishing Spaces In Between

Pause for a moment and notice your breathing. You are inhaling and exhaling and then there is a space in between. There is a rhythm to your breathing. It can feel wonderful to breathe deeply and notice the breath flow naturally in your body. It has a naturally calming and replenishing effect, on both the physical and energetic state of your being.

Conversations in flow have a similar rhythm. There is the inhale, the call, the question, and then there is the exhale, the response. And in great conversation there is also the silence, the pause, the crack in the conversation that allows for fresh insights to come in and old thinking to leave. Imagine yourself breathing without pausing in between. That's the kind of breathing you have when you are running, for example. There may still be short pauses, but it's mostly a continuous breathing in and out. We are on a track, we are focused, and we are working out. You may even notice an "I am in charge" quality to this kind of breathing without pause. I breathe in. I breathe out. I breathe in. I breathe out.

Conversely, when we are at rest, there is this pause after every outbreath, as if the body is processing something without our doing anything about it. The pause after the outbreath has a quality of letting go. Similarly, in a conversation, pauses can be helpful, to let new insights in, and old thinking go.

Our crocodiles dislike the pause. It's always all hands on deck. Go, go, go. In a conversation, being in the groan zone—the part of the conversation where we have stated the issue we are talking about and we haven't come to a conclusion yet, that creative middle—is where our crocodile is most uncomfortable.

Being in the groan zone, we can choose to not give in to the restlessness of the crocodile, but instead just relax. This doesn't mean we tune out and go to sleep. No, we stay alert, we are fully present in the here and now, but we don't do anything for a moment. We let the present moment be the present moment.

In some conversations, we are in the groan zone for quite a while. In others, it's only a few moments. And there is the groan zone within the groan zone. There is the time in conversation where we haven't landed on a conclusion yet. And there is the space in between you and me talking. I like to think about this as the macro- and the micro-groan zone. The macro-groan zone is the time in a conversation where we don't know yet, where we are exploring together what the issue is, what it is about, and what different ways there may be to address it. The micro-groan zone is the space in between us talking.

The energy we bring to the macro- and micro-groan zones is similar. We simply rest. We exhale. We let the dust settle. We connect to a deeper place inside of us and the other. And we let that deeper place speak. The groan zone is a time for intuition to make itself heard. It's a time for us to take an inventory of our thinking and ask ourselves: Is this still true? Is this thought still helpful? We let go of our old ideas to make space for new ones. We exhale and rest. The more we rest, the more invigorating the inhale will be. The more we really pause, the more we are able to take in the insights that come from the depth of our being—theirs and ours.

Great conversations also happen in the spaces in between. Maybe the greatest parts of conversations happen from these spaces, which are gateways to the great stillness that underlies it all. Informed by this great stillness, we become creative, kind, wise, compassionate. Disconnected from it, we tend to run around in our heads, trying to force solutions and not seeing issues from a deeper, truer perspective. Then we see only what our crocodiles see: problem, danger, fix it now, problem, danger, fix it now. For crocodiles, conversations are forced drudgery. From the stillness of the owl, conversations are simply ways to listen together to what is true and give voice and action to that truth.

## Leadership Practice

*Notice your inbreath and outbreath. Now also notice the space after the outbreath. Allow yourself to dwell there for a few moments without forcing it. What is it like to rest in the pauses between your breaths? What qualities come online in you as you rest there? What would it be like if you also brought these qualities to the conversations you have today?*

## PRACTICE 56
### Multiple Perspectives

"THERE WILL BE an answer, let it be, let it be." My crocodiles are in violent disagreement with this idea. Instead, I need to push harder, think more, make myself busier, try to manipulate the other person into doing what I need them to do...and the list goes on. In conversation with another, breakthroughs often occur when we least expect it. Somehow, somebody says something we hadn't thought about yet. An idea flashes into our minds that clarifies things. We see a new connection between things we hadn't noticed before. We recognize a new pattern.

Conversations can be highly co-creative when we let them be. It's like we are creating art together. We are together in *intention*, in what we would like to see happen, and in *attention*, being deeply grounded in presence, unconditional love. Grounded in presence, we are watching and participating in the conversation simultaneously. We watch insights show up, hear them from the other, and speak them as they come through us. An issue comes to life as we bring our attention to it. Have you ever noticed that a seemingly mundane topic, like a business plan or a project update, can turn into a highly engaging exchange that leaves you feeling nourished and full of new ideas? This co-creative process has very few requirements. Basically, it asks us to be in intention and to be present, while letting the series of ensuing present moments take care of the rest. We keep leaning in, we keep going deeper, with the intention of seeing what is true about the issue at hand. And as we see more clearly, it becomes more obvious what our choices are.

I sometimes think that creating, like writing, is not so much about creating from nothing. It is putting pieces that already existed—ideas, insights, present moments, energy—together in a way that is tangible. Creation is making the intangible tangible. In great conversations, we put words to things that didn't have words before. We build on top of each other's ideas. We draw new connections. In great conversations, we connect deeply with each other and with each other's perspectives and ideas.

One crocodilian misperception that we heal as we give ourselves to a conversation is that we need to keep defending our egoic identities. In conversation, a big one is "I am right." From presence, we don't worry about this. We ask: What if both of us were right, then what would we see? What if there were a different way of seeing this that I hadn't considered before? What if...?

Asking "what if" opens the door to new possibilities and relaxes our compulsive crocodilian need to be right. Having a "what if" mindset, we make no idea wrong. We keep building on each other. We keep exploring and building until we know it's time to make some choices. We will know when that time is.

Co-creation starts with the intention to develop a common view of what is true about the situation. We step into each other's eyes for a moment and see it from the other's perspective. We also take a "systems view" and take a look at what this situation looks like with all of us in it. We practice this, deliberately taking on three camera views—one looking through our own eyes, the second looking from the other's eyes, and the third one looking from the ceiling to all of us involved in the issue at hand. What is true from my perspective? What is true from their perspective? What is true from the system's perspective? We keep switching angles, while staying grounded in truth, and ask ourselves: What if all perspectives were true, then what would we see?

When we look this way, the universe turns into a university. We take every perspective as helpful in seeing the deeper truth about things. This is not something we force. It is something that we let happen while actively staying in intention, focused on our purpose; staying in attention, grounded in presence; staying open to all perspectives to see greater truth and ready to act on it when the insight and the time is there.

## Leadership Practice

*Reflect on an issue you are facing. Practice taking multiple perspectives on it: What is true from my point of view? What is true from their point of view? What is true about the situation from the system's point of view? Let the insights emerge; don't force them.*

*Do this same practice again, now when you are in the midst of a conversation. How does this help you to see more clearly? How does it help you to be more creative and more connected with the other?*

## PRACTICE 57
### Free to Commit

NATURE IS COMMITTED. The sun rises and sets at a predictable time. Ebb becomes flow. Our inhale becomes the exhale and our heart keeps beating steadily throughout it all. Gravity is always here. There is so much in nature that we can rely on. This gives us a sense of stability, orientation, and faith. We know tomorrow the sun will rise again. We know we can always plant our feet on the earth. It will be there for us.

The word *commitment* comes from Latin *committere*, which means "to join together, engage, place in the keeping of, entrust, bring about." When we commit to our lives, we join together with nature. We take a stand for what we value and let nature do its part, being there for us every step of the way. Similarly, we join together with another through conversation. We make a promise to the other to do something and do what we say. We request from the other to do something for us. We join together in a commitment to be here for each other and walk these steps of the journey together.

Creating commitment requires conscious attention. The crocodile doesn't know about natural rhythms. It would schedule ebb and flow at the same time if it suited its timing better. Or it avoids commitment altogether. Under the influence of the crocodile, we will try to force people to give us what we want. As opposed to asking a clean question, "In order to accomplish XYZ, I request that you do A by B time. Will you do that?" we say things like "I assume you'll do that," "I am sure you understand that . . ." or even more aggressively, "Have you taken care of this yet?" while the other person hadn't given us their promise yet. Or we fudge our promises and say things like "maybe," "at some point," or "sure."

A clean commitment is a contract. It joins people together to realize a common purpose. We join our individual wills into a common one to create something together. We come together to dedicate a portion of our time and attention. How do we make sure our commitment is real?

We can use our body as a tool. Our body is here for as long as we live. You could say our body is committed to our being here. It shows up every day. We can use the grounding energy of our body to make quality commitments. Literally taking our seat, we can rest our attention on our sits bones and reflect: How committed am I to this? What can I really commit to? What am I ready to put myself into the hot seat for, knowing there will be other priorities vying for my time and attention? Taking our seat is energizing. It helps us to feel rooted in intention. Without it, we may get lost in the spinning of our head and the endless pros and cons our dualistic mind comes up with. Taking our seat, we make an unconditional commitment to something. We say we are going to do it, and we will.

Grounded in our seat, we further energize our commitment by checking in with the heart. How does my heart see this commitment? What do I really want to give to this? What feels right that I give? What is the energy that I will bring? With the heart committed, we assume a sense of responsibility and care for our commitment. We activate our caring energy. We say to each other, verbally or nonverbally, "You can count on me, I will be here to care for this."

Grounded in our seat, connected with our hearts, we are ready to make the third level of commitment—from our head. We commit to keeping our head clear, our choices wise, and our actions firm, no matter what happens. With single pointed focus we stay on task, no matter what happens.

A friend of mine describes this sometimes as a "full body YES." Before she commits to something she checks in with her body and holds the question "does this commitment feel right for me right now?" If her body feels heavy, lethargic, or even wants to run away as she thinks about this commitment, that's a great caution flag that there is something out of alignment. If the body feels energized, excited, or lighter, those reactions support a clean, clear step forward into commitment.

This doesn't mean that a commitment is for always. Life can happen; things can happen that ask us to reconsider our commitments. In that case, we come back to our commitment number 1: to be present. From presence, we will know when it's time to renegotiate our commitments, taking care of people and the task at hand in the best possible way.

Commitment, from the crocodile's perspective, feels like a burden we need to carry, or a shield we put up to protect ourselves against the uncertainty of life. From the perspective of unconditional love and presence, commitment turns into a celebration. We celebrate that we have the freedom to commit, to join with nature and the other to build something new. Freedom leads to true commitment, control only to coercion. Being free, we commit with delight to spending a portion of our time and attention on what is being asked of us.

## Leadership Practice

*Think of a conversation you are in. What request can you make of the other? How open are you on a scale from 1 to 10 to their response?*

*What promise can you make to them? Reflect for a moment how your promise feels from the perspective of your seat, your heart, and your head.*

# PRACTICE 58
## Zero Pedestals

WE JUST AS easily give power away as we take it from others when our crocodile is in charge. "Jim is about to join us," one team member says. The room becomes quiet, people start looking a bit tense, and when Jim joins, the open conversation they were having just a minute ago has degenerated into a kind of performance where people are trying to say the right thing, as opposed to being authentic and relaxed. You guessed it: Jim is their boss, and people's crocodiles put Jim on a pedestal. He has the power to promote or fire, doesn't he? Afraid of how Jim may grade them, people put on their performance masks.

Observing myself and other "bosses" in team meetings, I can feel the opposite dynamic as well, where I try to take away people's power, with my crocodile believing that they are less than me, putting myself on a pedestal. Why would my crocodile want to believe that anyone is less than me? I can control them more easily. This gives me an inflated sense of superiority, of "better than." What may be other reasons why we are interested in a better-than image? Mine is that it gives me a sense of safety. Being above the "riffraff," I don't have to deal with all the human complexities. I simply dictate what needs to happen. It's so much simpler than dealing with life directly, thinks the crocodile. Looking a little deeper, I see that my sense of superiority stems from a sense of inferiority. I believe I am not up to par with life to deal with it as it comes. I deny my own power to deal with life as it comes, and create a fantasy self-image that I believe will magically control life for me. Better than, I believe I am the great puppeteer who can force life to my will. How is that working for me? Not great. People and things don't like to be controlled. In the end, they won't. And it takes a lot of energy to keep propping myself up to stay on a pedestal, and keep polishing my image of better than.

What would it be like if we no longer put anyone on a pedestal, including ourselves? What would become possible for us? The word *power* comes from the Latin word *posse*, which means "to be able to." What would we be able to be and do standing in our true power?

No longer giving our power away to our bosses—or other people and things we have put on a pedestal, like communities, money, and status—we discover inner freedom, an inner flexibility to be and respond from our highest truth, rather than from some idea of who we should be, like the Subservient One, Capable One, Nice One, or Special One. We are here, now, resting in presence, as presence, and we bring that energy to bear to what's in front of us, rather than giving in to fear-based hallucinations that have us contort ourselves and put on some kind of mask. We feel a higher power coming through us that guides our being, words, and actions. And we notice that power also in others. It's not even ours or theirs, it's simply here. We can trust that. We become empowered when we see that a higher power is coming through all of us—free of charge, and independent of our role in life.

When we are no longer making ourselves more or less than, life becomes simple. We are simply here. One day we are the boss, the next day we are reporting to someone. One day we are asked to make decisions that affect many, another day we are receiving the impact of someone else's decision. We stay equanimous through it all. We realize our equality. We are all one in presence, one in our access to a higher power. We free ourselves from our insecurities that needed us to be better than. We know we are fully equipped, by a higher power, to take care of things as they are needed. We know that. And we know other people have access to that same power. It's not ours, it doesn't belong to any one of us. It's simply here. We get to apply it from it, from our different stations in life.

As opposed to asking ourselves, "How can I make them do this?" or, "How can I make them like me?" we ask: "Guide me to serve from my station now. Let me be an instrument for what needs to happen now."

We empower ourselves by living and leading without any pedestals. No money, no celebrity, no boss, no one can distract us from standing in the higher power that comes through us. We let go of any need to control anything or anyone. We no longer need to have power over, because the real power comes through all of us. That power orchestrates and creates the order that is needed now. We feel confident that we have what it takes to be with and work with anything that comes our way. We don't need to make ourselves lower than or higher than anyone or anything. We are up to the task. We are up to life.

## Leadership Practice

*Who do you put on a pedestal? How do you give your power away to them?*

*With whom do you put yourself on a pedestal? How do you try to force them to do what you want them to do?*

*Who would you be without any of these pedestals? How would you lead and live differently?*

## PRACTICE 59
### Free of Judgment, Full of Appreciation

THE WILDFLOWERS THAT have come up through the cracks in the concrete behind our garage are just as beautiful and vibrant as those I see on hikes in the mountains. The flowers are expressing freely what they are made of, no matter what their external circumstances are.

We humans are wired somewhat differently. Instead of simply being with our surroundings, we tend to judge our surroundings reflexively as "good," "bad," or "indifferent" to us. We let ourselves get enmeshed with our surroundings, by spending some of our precious time and attention judging others. We enmesh ourselves by judging others. We *should* others all day long: They should behave this way. They shouldn't have done that. They should be different. Our judgmental mind never seems to stop. We always have a next judgment ready to be fired off. This resistance to what is takes tremendous effort. We can get so lost in our judgments of others that we forget ourselves and what we came here to do. Unlike the flowers behind our garage, we forget to bloom, too busy telling the concrete how it should be different.

As with all mental faculties, there is value in judgment. I would call that discernment—to be able to see what works and what doesn't, what is effective and what is not, what is safe and what is unsafe, what is in harmony and what is not. Paradoxically, the freer we become from crocodilian judgment, the clearer our mind becomes, and therefore, the more we are able to discern what is needed now. We can use our discernment to be and act from our highest truth, rather than using it as a knife that our crocodile wields to go to battle against reality as it is.

Check it out for yourself. How does it feel to judge someone? Do you like it? What is the impact on your sense of fulfillment, creativity, and integrity? Chances are judgment depletes you from the inside. It chews up your energy. Why? Because judging others, we invest energy in the expectation we have of others. The more we expect from others, the more we open ourselves to inevitable disappointment and resentment. Judging others, we give energy to our hidden agenda that is invested in their changing. Truth be told, this rarely works. People cannot be coerced, at least not in a sustainable way. The more we judge, the more we put ourselves in resistance to who people are now. This takes tremendous energy. And this energy is wasted. It doesn't lead to anything but frustration, broken relationships, and ineffectiveness. The costs of judgment are staggering.

We don't only judge others. We judge ourselves also. All day long. We put one expectation on top of the other. Am I effective enough? Nice enough? Rich enough? Successful enough? Learning enough? Generous enough? Impactful enough? Wise and compassionate enough? Am I enough? We are Don Quixote lost in a battle with ourselves. We hope one day we will finally arrive at the self-image that will make us feel enough. Unfortunately, we are working toward some fantasy perfect state that we will never reach.

Is it true that we are not enough now? Who says? Who would we be without the thought of enough or not enough? In the end these are just conceptualizations of reality and not reality itself. The more we let go of self-judgment, the more we are restored to a natural relationship with ourselves and others. The more we see through the whole mental construct of having to be someone, the more we connect to the well-being, peace, and joy that we are and always will be. The word *relationship* comes from Latin *relatio*, which means "bringing back, restoring." Free from judgment, we are restored to a true relationship with ourselves. No longer clouded by self-judgment, we see ourselves for who we are and always have been—presence, unconditional love, that for which we have no words.

Free from self-judgment, we become ready to be restored to true relationship with others as well. As we see through our own self-critical hallucinations and discover more of our true selves, we recognize the true self in others also. We see how our judgments about them are really our own interpretations of reality driven by our fear-based need to control others to be as we want them to be, as opposed to daring to be with them exactly as they are now. What would it be like if we no longer judged anyone else? How would this free us up to connect more to our own energy and to see people for who they truly are—loving, lovable, and loved, just as we are?

This doesn't mean we throw out the baby with the bathwater. We retain our powers of discernment—seeing clearly what works and what doesn't; what is effective, safe, and in harmony and what isn't. We act based upon this discernment, as freely and as beautifully as the flowers behind our garage are blooming at the moment. Paradoxically, we become much more grounded in our decisions, the more we let go of judgment. No longer clouded by judgment, of ourselves and of others, we see clearly what is here now and how to be and act accordingly.

No longer judging others, a space opens in which we naturally begin to appreciate them. Our minds and hearts cleaned from judgment, we connect with the tremendous potential and beauty in everyone.

Judgment is a deeply engrained habit for most of us. Therefore, having some daily practice to loosen its grip on our minds can be helpful. With some teams we practice "Picture Moments," where we reflect for a few seconds a few times a day on who we appreciate on the team and why. This practice chips away at judgment and replaces it with appreciation and gratitude.

What would happen if instead of judging someone, you appreciated them? What becomes possible for you then?

---

## Leadership Practice

*Think of someone you judge. What judgment have you put on the other person?*

*Is there something this judgment is protecting you from?*

*What do you feel when you have your judgmental thoughts?*

*Who would you be without this judgment?*

*What do you appreciate about the other person and yourself? What are you grateful for?*

# PRACTICE 60
## Hula-Hoop Relationships

TREES IN THE forest stand both alone and together. Each has its own intricate root system, and together with the other trees they form a tightly connected ecosystem where nutrients and other vital resources are exchanged freely. Healthy relationships are like a forest. We each stand in our own roots—our values, needs, intentions, and actions—and we are in dynamic connection with those around us.

If we try to be the roots of others, forcing our ideas and beliefs on them, we lose balance. We can remember this as staying in our own Hula-Hoop. As soon as we try to get into someone else's, we both fail. I drop mine and I disturb yours.

This sounds simple, and yet much of crocodilian conditioning is geared toward our getting into someone else's hoop. The crocodile doesn't trust us enough to address life's challenges standing on our own two feet. It thinks we'll have a better chance if we control the ecosystem we are part of. We get quite sophisticated being in others' business—for example, by giving unsolicited advice, micromanaging, blaming, judging, manipulating, and rescuing, to name a few of our favorite crocodilian control mechanisms.

We know we're in someone else's business when we feel out of balance. The hoop of our energy and action is not spinning the way we know it can. We feel contracted, stressed out, on guard, overworked, worried, and obsessed. Our mind quickly becomes unsettled trying to keep track of everyone else's Hula-Hoop.

Staying in our own business does not mean we isolate ourselves. We stand on our own two feet, we touch the ground of presence that unites us. We feel the presence, unconditional love, that is within us and them. We rest in that presence while we are with them. We open ourselves to feel what they may feel, without getting lost in their feelings. We simply see it as information that we can respond to from the highest truth that we have realized. We listen deeply to what they are saying and share openly what we are about. And we are sensitive to the context. For example, we may not share our deepest secret with someone standing next to us at Starbucks, or even with a teammate. Grounded in presence, we see clearly what is called for to be said and what is not.

From time to time, we may encounter some turbulence relating with others. Sometimes one or both of us has a crocodilian flare-up. In these moments, we can simply pause, and literally feel our own two feet again. What is true for me now? How can I stay true to my highest intention in this moment, no matter what the other person may do or not do?

However contrary to our feelings it may seem, it is not our job to get the other person out of their crocodilian reaction. Being grounded in presence, we simply watch any crocodilian reactivity empty out. This may be the greatest contribution we make to both people in the relationship. Especially for those of us who grew up being sensitive, and possibly played the rescuer or villain role in the family of origin, this can be quite challenging. I remember the slogan "Do what you don't want to do and don't do what you want to do" in these moments. My crocodile will scream, *Go fix it, go fix it*. Emotional heat will build up in my body. As opposed to trying to relieve the discomfort by giving in to it, I take a step back, breathe deeply, and do what my crocodile really doesn't want me to do: I am still. I rest. I wait and let the dust inside of me settle. Once I feel clear again, I may say something to continue the conversation.

All of this can happen in a few seconds, or it may take longer. Sometimes we may need to cool off, take a break, and come back to the conversation later. Don't fall for the crocodile's false sense of urgency. Remember, for our crocodile, every upset feels like a threat to its survival that needs to be dealt with immediately. No time like the present, yells the crocodile. Go fix it now!

Resting in presence, we see all this as a mere cloud in the sky of awareness. It may be a thundercloud, but it's a cloud nevertheless. Thunderclouds help clear the air. Just let it happen. We have nothing to lose. We will be the sky, presence, before, during, and after. Nothing real can be threatened and nothing unreal exists.

We bring to our relationships a sky-like presence, no matter what happens. We stand firm, like the tree, yet deeply connected to everything and everyone around us.

---

## Leadership Practice

*How can you stay more in your Hula-Hoop today? What will be the impact on yourself, the other, and your effectiveness?*

# PART 7

## Helping Others Grow

# PRACTICE 61
## Coaching Intention—Being Here Now

THINK OF SOMEONE who has helped you grow. What do you feel toward them? Maybe a sense of gratitude, warmth, respect, possibly even awe. Helping each other grow is one of the beautiful ways we relate to each other as human beings. The word *coaching* comes from Hungarian *kocsi*, which means "carriage," the horse-drawn vehicle that helped us get where we wanted to go a hundred-plus years ago. Coaching is about helping others realize their objectives. Growth Leadership coaching is one specific method of coaching geared toward helping the coachee grow more into who they truly are and apply that in their lives and leadership. It goes beyond guiding someone through a challenge. It is about helping others find the lessons in the challenges that life presents them with.

How do we coach others this way? It starts with us grounding ourselves in a powerful intention. If we don't, we are likely to be seduced by any of the many ploys with which our crocodile will try to distract us. Coaching is about helping them, not about helping us, even though we will also grow when we coach, sharing the experience with them. For the crocodile, *everything is about me*. In that sense, coaching is a radical act. It's not about me, it's about them.

Despite our best intentions, the crocodile will try to use a coaching session to shore up our identity. Look at me, says the crocodile. I am so wise, and such a great coach! And look at all these breakthroughs I helped people have. Coachees cry in my sessions, I must be a very good coach!

The crocodile is in heaven when we give in to this kind of self-aggrandizing self-talk. Let me ask a really tough question...That will teach them. Or maybe I should impress them with my analysis and understanding of the situation. Better yet, I should give them advice!

To tame our crocodilian thinking before a coaching session, it helps to give it a name. I like to think of it as the FINISH (Fixing It Now I Superhero) crocodile. This stands in stark contrast with a much more grounded coaching intention we can have.

At the beginning of a coaching conversation, we go back to basics. We come back to presence. We ask ourselves, on a scale from 1 to 10, how present am I now? We take a few deep conscious breaths into the belly and allow ourselves to fully come back to the here and now. From this space of presence, we may connect with our deeper coaching intention. What is our intention for this coaching conversation? How can we come from the highest truth we have realized about ourselves?

Being present, we inspire the coachee to connect to the ground of their being, presence, unconditional love. We coach like Michelangelo carved the beautiful statue of David in Florence. You may recall him saying that "I saw an angel in the stone and I carved to set it free." We become angel carvers. We remind the coachee of their pure potential, and help them let go of all the stone that keeps them stuck in smallness—the mindsets and behaviors that are limiting them—so they can make space for, identify, and practice ones that are more aligned with their essence—their highest truth. In coaching we set a container for truth finding.

We can't find the truth for the coachee; the coachee will have to find this for themselves. We can ask questions, we can be with them, but we cannot tell them what it is. If we tell them, the coachee is far less likely to embody the learnings. "Oh, that was interesting," the coachee may think at the end of receiving advice. To truly help the coachee, we intend them to find their own answers. We are there to question their answers so they can find deeper answers that are more closely aligned with their true essence.

We ground ourselves in the energy of LOVE—Letting Others Voluntarily Evolve. We are here to help the coachee have their own realizations, in their own time. Especially this last bit—in their own time— is a challenge for our crocodile, who needs instant gratification. The time is right when it is, and not before. This goes contrary to a lot of our other business activities, where most things have to be done yesterday. We cannot force a human to develop. People develop in their own time.

We are there to be open, present, and loving, no matter what the coachee is doing. We transmit an energy of unconditional love, a pointer to the very essence we are helping the coachee uncover. Notice how different this is from the let-me-fix-you crocodile. Simply this, seeing the coachee with love, with kind eyes, often much kinder than they see themselves, can help the coachee relax and grow.

I am here to be present. Not to my time, but their time. As a coach, we are simply here, committed to providing the most catalyzing space possible for the other to find their own truth. That's what we anchor in. I am here now, creating a clean space for you to look at yourself, and to discover more of who you truly are.

***

## Leadership Practice

*What is your intention coaching others? What would happen if you let go of any and all Fixing-It-Now-I-Superhero FINISH tendencies? What if you adopted a LOVE—Letting Others Voluntarily Evolve—mindset?*

# PRACTICE 62
## The Owl's 5Qs and the Crocodile's 5Cs of Coaching

D O YOU FEEL ready to coach someone? You may wonder: Where do I start? How do I make sure I am offering the best possible coaching experience to the coachee?

Think of people who have coached you effectively. Chances are you remember them because they challenged you, they helped you see the bigger picture, helped you become aware of different ways of seeing the situation, supported you in your sense of confidence and self-acceptance, and maybe they asked a question that has stayed with you all these years. Reflecting on others who have coached us effectively, we may notice some patterns—there are very specific qualities that make coaches great.

I remember them as the 5Qs—five quotients, capacities that great coaches have. The simple act of reminding myself of these capacities activates them in me. They are: Meaning Quotient (MQ), Emotion Quotient (EQ), Intelligence Quotient (IQ), Intuition Quotient (NQ), and Contentment Quotient (CQ). Let's explore each of these in turn. As we go through them, reflect on how you already have this capacity. Also think about how you may be able to further develop it.

- *Meaning Quotient (MQ)*: We help the coachee see the bigger picture of the situation. We help them zoom out and see beyond the minutiae of the current challenge. We may ask: How do you want to look back at this situation when you retire? How is this situation a teacher for you? How can you use this situation to build the legacy you would like to leave?

- *Emotion Quotient (EQ)*: We use emotions as advisors and not as masters. We listen to emotions and see what information they contain, without becoming entangled in them. We practice emotional mastery. When a dense emotion shows up, we take a deep breath and come back to the balcony, sky awareness, and notice the emotion simply as a cloud in the unchanging sky of our awareness. We may inquire: How do you feel? What do you sense this feeling is telling you? What does the part of you that is feeling this want for you?

- *Intelligence Quotient (IQ)*: We use our thinking mind to become clear and meticulous about the challenge at hand. What is a concrete example of this challenge? What happened? What are the facts? What are your assumptions and interpretations? What old, conditioned beliefs are in play here? Who would you be without these stories? And we stay true to the time commitment for the coaching conversation. It has a clear beginning, middle and end, and we are skillfully bringing process and discipline to ensure we do our work in the time we have.

- *Intuition Quotient (NQ)*: So we don't repeat IQ, we call it NQ, iNtuition quotient. We tune in to intuition, grounding in the presence that we are, and let the stillness in us speak. We let ourselves be guided by a higher power that comes through us that goes beyond the conceptual mind and uses the conceptual mind to express it. We let ourselves be guided by ideas and images that don't feel like they come from our rational mind. Sometimes we call it a "gut sense" or an "inner knowing." It may feel like the ideas come through us rather than from within us. We tune in to that to know what question to ask next and where to focus the conversation. We learn to enjoy and trust intuition as a good friend.

- *Contentment Quotient (CQ)*: Throughout it all, we stay grounded in our essence, the ground of our being: presence, unconditional love. Whatever the coachee brings up, whatever emotions get triggered, we stay grounded in the clear sky of our awareness, seeing all of it as clouds in the sky. We remain detached and yet very involved. The more detached we are as the sky, the more we are able to relate deeply to everything the coachee is going through, as we know we don't need to fix it. It is by definition a passing phenomenon, and an invitation for learning and care. Deep down we know that all is well, and we transmit this energy to the coachee.

Just before a coaching conversation, or even during, we tune into these 5Qs, like looking at our inner dashboard to activate these energies in us. Activating them will help create a container in which we do our best work. Questions and insights come naturally as we are grounded in these 5Qs.

Imagine being a coachee who is feeling stuck in a problem. How would it help you if your coach inspired you to see the bigger picture (MQ)? Let's say you felt very upset about it. What would it be like if your coach was staying calm, yet empathetic, and helped you distill the wisdom from your feelings (EQ)? Maybe you didn't see the forest for the trees. How would it help if a coach helped you see the pattern and how this event is an example of it (IQ)? What would it be like if somehow you learned to trust your intuition as you sense the coach is trusting his (NQ)? Finally, how would it be if you were met each time with the energy of *all is well* by your coach (CQ)? How might this help you relax and connect to your own sense of presence, contentment, and wisdom?

All the while, our crocodile will want to interrupt the conversation wherever it can. It will try to hijack our 5Q intelligence and distort it with fear-based thinking and feeling. To keep an eye on the crocodile during a coaching, we name our crocodilian coaching efforts the *5Cs*: *Crisis, Craziness, Criticism, Calculation,* and *Concern.* Instead of helping us to see the bigger picture (MQ), the crocodile will want us to believe we are in an all-consuming *crisis.* As opposed to staying emotionally balanced (EQ), it will try to make us *crazy,* burying us under heaps of difficult feelings and getting totally enmeshed with the coachee's drama. It will use our intellect to *criticize* and make wrong, as opposed to helping to discern patterns with detachment (IQ). It will approach the coachee like a spreadsheet, letting *if this then that* thinking dominate, relying on *calculating* logic at the expense of intuitive insight (NQ). And finally, it will join the coachee in their *concern,* overwhelm and worry, as opposed to resting in presence, unconditional love, and transmitting that all is well (CQ).

What will become possible for you as coach, as you let your innate 5Q capacities be turned on a bit more today?

---

## Leadership Practice

*Reflect on the 5Qs: Meaning (MQ), Emotion (EQ), Intelligence (IQ), Intuition (NQ), and Contentment (CQ). Which of these is your strongest quality as a coach? Which one is your weakest? Which one would you like to develop more?*


*Which of the crocodile's coaching 5Cs do you need to be aware of in yourself (Crisis, Craziness, Criticism, Calculation, Concern)?*

## PRACTICE 63
## MQ (Meaning)—Seeing the Bigger Picture

L IFE AND LEADERSHIP can seem like a series of hoops we have to jump through. From this vantage point, there is little joy. Maybe we get short snippets of momentary satisfaction when we cross something off our to-do list, achieve something we value, or when we have been able to stave off one crisis or another.

There is a different way of seeing life and leadership. The inner journey shifting our perspective from "this then that" to something more expansive, more life giving, more joyful, is one we help our coachees make. To be able to do that, we ourselves first have to have had a glimpse of the power that gets unleashed from consciously shifting our perspective. In what follows, I invite you to explore for yourself: What happens if I shift my perspective? What happens when I see things differently?

How we see things is a function of our conditioning. *We don't see things as they are, we see things as we are*, it says in the Talmud. Believing in scarcity, we will see an upset as possible collapse of our financial stability. Having bought into the story of abandonment, we will interpret many relationship dynamics as someone leaving us or validating that we "have" them for another day. Believing the myth that "I am special," we see changes as opportunities for self-aggrandizement or, conversely, for being ridiculed. Our inner stories have a decisive impact on how we see the world if we let them.

We can relax our stories and open to a bigger perspective that is more truthful by challenging two common assumptions: what is happening now is about our identity; and what is happening now is happening in isolation, disconnected from everything that happened before and will happen after. Let's explore this further.

Let's say you didn't get your promotion and you're upset about it, so much so that you can't stop thinking about it. Is it true that you should have gotten the promotion? Well, to make you feel safe, important, validated—all egoic identities—it should have happened. Without any of these identities you may touch some freedom and lightness in you. How would you be with this challenge if you didn't attach to any identity? Well, maybe you'd see it as something that happened. Maybe there is something for you to learn and you'd move on from there.

Let's examine the second assumption—this event is happening in isolation, meaning it's the beginning, middle, and end of your world, all at the same time. Is this true? No, of course not. You didn't get this promotion and you have gotten other jobs in the past and you will likely get new ones in the future. Not getting this promotion is part of your life's journey. It's neither the beginning, middle, nor end. When you take a step back you may notice how this event, as part of your history, has something to teach you. Maybe you are gaining awareness of a bigger pattern in your life? How often have you become totally obsessed with something else before? How would you live your life without this sense of obsession?

Taking a step back from the situation, we free ourselves from two basic crocodilian stories: I am this separate identity, and this is the end of my world. Who would you be without these stories?

Unleashing the bonds of our small crocodilian thinking, we open ourselves to a bigger perspective. We access this bigger perspective by asking different questions. What can this upset teach you? What potentially limiting patterns in you does it point to? What would happen if you kept giving in to this crocodilian narrative for the next year, three years, five years? Who would you be in five years' time without this narrative? How is this upset helping you to shed some identities that are no longer serving you, like being the Nice One, the Competent One, the Special One, or the Rescuer?

How is your upset part of a bigger trend we are facing as humanity? What pattern does it point to in your family, in your generation, in your company? What would it be like if you were able to make a small dent in this pattern, not only for yourself, but also for the people around you? Then, how would you lead through this challenge differently?

Questioning our assumptions of separateness and isolation, we start to see we are part of a bigger whole.

Seeing a challenge as part of a bigger picture gives us energy. When we find that an upset is an invitation to extend more of our true selves—unconditional love, presence, peace—it can unleash energy in us. It's as if we open the floodgates that our crocodiles had worked so hard to build, and let the light, the caring, and fortitude of presence in. We open our floodgates by shifting our perspective from everything being about number one, little me, to seeing that we are part of the infinite whole and contributing from that life-giving vantage point. As Walt Whitman wrote: *What verse will you contribute?*

## Leadership Practice

*For a challenge you have, notice any crocodilian stories you are telling yourself about it.*

*How are the two common assumptions "it's about my identity" and "this is the end of the world" part of these stories?*

*What becomes possible for you when you relax these stories? What is a different story you can tell yourself? How are you growing through this situation? How can you contribute differently now, given your wider vantage point?*

# PRACTICE 64
## EQ—Being with Our Feelings

OUR FEELINGS, LIKE clouds in the sky, come and go. One moment we feel happy, the next slightly anxious or maybe even a bit sad, and then we may feel enthusiasm for something—our inner kaleidoscope keeps producing new feeling states. How can we best be with our emotions, both our own and those of our coachees?

Our crocodile attaches big meaning to everything we feel. If we are excited, this means we have arrived and should hold on to that feeling. Feeling sad is unsafe and we should get rid of it. Being angry is a no-no, so we should act it out or suppress it. Our crocodile tries to control our feeling states all day long. That takes a lot of energy.

From the vantage point of presence, our feeling states are exactly that—states of feeling that, like clouds, are passing through the sky of our awareness. We may see the clouds, but we don't identify with them. We *have* feelings. We *are not* our feelings. We may notice that many of them, especially fear, anxiety, anger, and shame, often have their roots in crocodilian hallucinations we are believing to be real. We get swept up by our stories and feel the anguish, pain, and hurt that come with them.

Inquiring into the feeling helps us be with them skillfully without being taken on a ride by them. What is this feeling telling me? Is this true? Who would I be without this story? The more we ask ourselves this question—who would I be without this story—the more we experience the peace, love, and joy that remain after we have scrubbed our self-limiting beliefs from our consciousness. The more we scrub away the false stories, the more we come in direct contact with the ground of our being—that place of stillness, peace, and joy that we all know we have, and yet don't always feel connected with.

This doesn't mean we will never experience sadness, anger, shame, or anxiety again. We just don't take it as personally. We remember that we are the sky in which these feeling states occur. We are the sky that includes the clouds, as opposed to being only the clouds themselves.

This is not to say that clouds have no value. They do. The clouds, our feelings, often contain helpful information. Just like a physical feeling of hot or cold, they can tell us what to pay attention to. Feeling sad, we may want to spend some time to grieve something or someone we have lost. Filled with anger, we can inquire into the boundary that was crossed and how we can take a stand for ourselves, without standing against others. Feeling scared, we may inquire what danger there is, beyond any danger to our sense of emotional identity. What do I need to pay attention to? What do I need to protect? Feeling excited, we may wonder: What is it that I am looking forward to, and how can I nourish this? Feeling love, I can let myself enjoy this feeling, paying attention to myself and the ones around me.

All the while, we realize feelings are not facts and that they are fleeting. A feeling cannot tell us what is true—although a feeling, especially a gut feeling, can point to what is true. We simply observe the feeling with detachment and draw our lessons from it.

Being with our coachee, we bring emotional maturity (EQ) by being aware of the feelings in the conversation—theirs as well as our own—and drawing lessons from them, without attaching to any of them. We don't serve the coachee by colluding in emotional drama. That only feeds the crocodilian fear-based thinking that this is somehow the end of the world, with the coachee at its center. We are with all emotions, without getting enmeshed in any of them. We inquire to see what information they have to give us.

And we stay open to all feelings. We may invite the coachee to give themselves permission to feel their feelings more deeply than they have until now. We may say something like "All your feelings are welcome here." We model for the coachee a way for them to relate to their own feelings by the way that we relate to their feelings.

Our crocodilian selves tend to want to suppress uncomfortable feelings, believing that we can't handle them. We may feel something difficult deep down and we try to make it go away and numb it, by aggressively acting it out—yelling, judging, dramatizing, and sarcasm are examples of this numbing strategy—or by telling ourselves a tranquilizing story, saying to ourselves that we are fine when we are not, that we are happy when we are sad, and that we are excited when we feel dread. These tranquilizers are not true. They take tremendous mental energy to make us believe that they are. Stuffing our feelings this way, we deepen our inner discord.

Instead of numbing our feelings, we can simply pause and say quietly to ourselves: "I am here for you. I am not going anywhere." We remind ourselves and our feelings that we are unchanging like the sky that encompasses everything. We welcome all parts of ourselves. Somehow by our welcoming our feelings, they tend to relax. They become lighter as they understand that they are not the end-all and be-all. The feeling energy relaxes its tunnel vision and opens up to the vast perspective it is part of—the infinite sky. We remind ourselves that who we are in essence, the sky, is infinitely bigger than our emotions.

If a difficult feeling stays for a while, we may ask ourselves a question my teacher Adyashanti likes to ask: What is the part in you that is not suffering while you are suffering? We can offer that part to the difficult feeling, be it our own or the coachee's, by being unconditional love, being presence. As we do so, we remind ourselves that we have this inner stability, this vast perspective inside of each of us, this inner sky that can hold every emotion, no matter how challenging. Being as anchored as the sky gives us the wherewithal to inquire into the feelings from a place of presence and stillness. We calmly inquire into the feelings without getting lost in them. We are here for them. Ready to listen to their stories, ready to learn, and then move on with our day.

---

## Leadership Practice

*Take a few deep breaths into the belly. Now allow yourself to feel what you are feeling at a deeper level. Rest your attention on one feeling, and on one place in your body that may feel contracted. What is this feeling and contraction telling you? What happens with the feeling when you allow yourself to relax with the feeling, being with it as vast presence, unconditional love?*

*The next time you notice a strong feeling, see if you can follow these steps in the moment. Breathe, notice the feeling in the body, ask the feeling what it is telling you, and allow yourself to let it be and relax. In short: breathe, notice, ask and be.*

# PRACTICE 65
## IQ—Discerning Truthful Perspective

OUR CROCODILES HAVE our minds racing. What about this? What about that? Never at rest, always looking to put out another fire. At crocodile speed, we are not wise. We don't see clearly. We exchange one story of what is happening with another one. Never pausing long enough to look and see what is really going on. With our minds racing, we start racing too. We start acting rashly, spinning, not sure which side is up. That's the bad news. The good news is that we can break this reactive pattern, in part by using our discerning intelligence. We can apply this whether we are coaching ourselves or someone else.

We activate discernment by paying attention to something constant, like the breath. Taking a few deep breaths into the belly calms our nervous system and helps to bring us back to reality. And then we can put our discerning intelligence to work. What is really going on? What is happening? Take a look. What is the challenge really? Not the drama that your crocodile makes it out to be, but what is really happening? What are the facts? What assumptions have you made? Are these assumptions true? Who would you be without these assumptions? We use our intellectual mind to bring us back to sanity. Discernment helps us place our challenges in a true perspective—not the exaggerated gloom and doom or Pollyanna reality that the crocodile would have us believe and act out from.

With greater clarity, we become ready to explore the next question. How have you responded so far? And what has been the impact of that? What has been the impact of your actions on three dimensions of reality: the I (self), the We (relationships), and the It (effectiveness)? If the crocodile has been in charge thus far, chances are that you (the I) feel stressed out; you have alienated some people (the We); and that you have taken unfocused, possibly rash, quick-fix actions (the It). Looking with discernment at what has been happening can be uncomfortable, especially if we carry around the identity that we need to have it all together at all times. Yet, looking with discernment frees our mind from a lot of crocodilian gunk. It becomes clear what is really going on, beyond all our stories about it.

Discernment leads to clarity. And clarity leads to wise, compassionate, and effective action. Once we are clear about what has really been going on, another question comes logically into view: How can you respond differently? Notice the precision in this question. It's not how can you respond? But how can you respond *differently*? We repeat a practice we touched on earlier: *Don't do what you want to do and do what you don't want to do*. In other words, don't follow the crocodile into its crazy confused logic and reactive patterns. Step out of it. Make a clear, deliberate choice to consider taking a different path.

To motivate us to take the bold step of acting differently, we may ask: What will be the impact on the I-, We-, and It-dimensions, if you followed this path rather than the crocodilian one? You may discover something like: I will feel alive knowing I gave my best and in integrity with my highest values. I will likely have deepened relationships with others and probably have taken some wise, focused actions that likely will have gotten me closer to my goal.

The crocodile is twenty-five times faster than our wise, logical owl mind and forty times less wise, according to neuroscience studies comparing our reptilian with our reasoning brain. Do we want to take the time to slow down enough to let clarity come? Or is it really so urgent that we need to force clarity now? Who is talking, the owl or the crocodile? Blinded by rush, we know we're in the tight grip of the crocodile. Patiently exploring how we could respond differently, in and of itself, will bring us closer to sanity. Simply pausing will free us from crocodilian reactivity and reconnect us with the stillness inside.

Letting that exploration play out, we naturally arrive at a closing part of our coaching exploration. What *will* you do? What do you commit to, in other words? Don't fall for the crocodilian temptation that it needs to fix everything yesterday. Simply ponder: What is the next wisest step you can take? What is it that you need to be doing now to make progress? What will you do, and by when? I often find such peace knowing what I need to do now. I will do it and trust that tomorrow the next step will be revealed. Remember that a mountain looks very different once you get closer to it. The same is true for working on a challenge. We get to know the challenge ever more deeply, the more we work on it, every step of the way. The wisest steps are often the ones that seem the smallest, including doing nothing and pausing for a while, and taking a look around to see where we are before moving on.

A beautiful way to close this discerning conversation would be to reflect on: How are you growing? Again, with discernment, what is something you can let go of—a mindset or behavior (a "from")—and what is something new you can build (a "to")?

---

## Leadership Practice

*Reflect on a challenge that you are facing and practice some discernment questions on it, for example:*

*What is really happening?*

*How have you responded so far?*

*What has been the impact of that on the I, We, and It?*

*How can you respond differently?*

*What may be the impact of that on the I, We, and It?*

*What will you do?*

*How are you growing?*

*Enjoy exploring the energy of discernment.*

# PRACTICE 66
## NQ—Woodcarver Intuition

G ROWTH IS NONLINEAR. Unexpected insights help us on our way. Where do they come from? How can we access these insights coaching ourselves and others? Enter our intuitive capacity. We all have it, and it's something mysterious to most of us. How is it that we know the right question to ask? How does that person know just what our conversation is really about? Our linear mind, often at first surprised by the insight, usually is able to catch up and explain after the fact why the intuitive insight was a helpful one. We can't connect the dots looking forward. We can, paraphrasing Steve Jobs, connect them looking backward.

How do we activate our intuitive capacity? There is an ancient poem that describes the mysterious process of intuition. It's called "The Woodcarver" and it tells the story of how a craftsman responds to a prince's inquiry about how he was able to make a beautiful piece of art, a bell stand. Here is an excerpt:

> Khing, the master carver, made a bell stand
> Of precious wood. When it was finished,
> All who saw it were astounded. They said it must be
> The work of spirits.
> The Prince of Lu said to the master carver:
> "What is your secret?"
> Khing replied: "I am only a workman:
> I have no secret. There is only this:
> . . .
>
> My own collected thought
> Encountered the hidden potential in the wood;
> From this live encounter came the work
> Which you ascribe to spirits."

The craftsman gives us clues about how to access our intuition. We need to collect our thoughts, or in other words, start with a clear *intention*. What is the highest intention I can have for this coaching conversation? What is it that I wish to contribute? Starting with a strong intention, our minds open, ready to meet insights, "the hidden potential in the wood." We can't force insights; they just show up. We meet them. How do we become ready to truly meet them? This is where the second ingredient of activating our intuition comes in. This is our *attention*—being here right now—fully present to this moment, ourselves, and the other person we are coaching. Being with a person in presence, we notice subtleties about them. What is their mood? What does their energy feel like? We tune in to the moment and discover whatever presents itself. We have a "live encounter," not a staged encounter.

Our crocodile says, "Yes, but last time you said this and it worked really well, why don't you try that again?" That is not being in a live encounter. Now we are giving our conceptual mind priority at the expense of opening up to the depth of our being, where intuition lives.

Coming back to the present moment, we let it inform us. Of course, our perception will be informed as well by our past. The woodcarver probably learned how to carve wood over many years of practice. He brought his practice to this moment. With his practiced skillfulness, he was able to translate the live encounter into the "work." As a coach, we can learn to listen for insights. Over time, we become better at discerning insight from crocodilian thinking. We learn to recognize the insights by the quiet they present themselves with. Our still small voice doesn't make a fuss. It's simply there, even if we don't listen to it. It may turn up its volume. Yet it stays grounded. And it usually doesn't provide any explanations. It's very much "well, this is how it is." We can learn to hold this intuitive clarity with humility. This is what's true for us and that doesn't mean it's true for everyone else.

As a coach, we learn to trust our intuition, as the woodcarver trusted the live encounter with the wood. We learn to pause and listen to it and make decisions based upon it. We learn to trust it to inform us what the next question may be. And we learn to listen to the coachee and let intuition guide us to the core of what is being said. We also hear what is not being said, the underlying story, that is ready to be heard.

Leading and living from intuition is rewarding, even beyond coaching conversations with others. We can choose to keep an ear open for intuition throughout the day and let it inform our choices. Oh, the adventure that the everyday becomes this way, living in a state of surrender to the little voice inside.

---

## Leadership Practice

*Take a few deep conscious breaths into the belly. Start noticing your breathing. Soften your gaze. Now set an intention for a coaching conversation you want to have, with yourself or with another. How would you like to show up? How would you like to contribute? Now allow yourself to just sit in silence, not doing anything for a minute or two. Just keep your focus on your intention. Relax and let any insights, however small, just appear. Listen to the still small voice inside of you. What are you learning?*

## PRACTICE 67
### CQ (Contentment)—Being and Bringing Peace

WE ARE THE first generation that is experiencing firsthand that we are destroying the planet. And we are the last generation that can do something about it," said one leader. Challenges abound; is it possible to still find peace in the midst of this?

It all depends on our perspective. Our thinking mind never finds lasting peace. It will always find another problem to solve, whether it's a conflict at work, a task that can be done better, or dealing with challenges at home, such as financial or relational issues, getting sick, aging, and dying. Life continues and our thinking is trying to keep up with it. That's a beautiful thing if you think about it deeply. Our thinking is helping us in so many ways. Just like our autonomous functions—like breathing and digesting—help us stay alive, our thinking mind helps us understand, relate, organize, create, and contribute. And yet, our thinking mind cannot get us to lasting peace—even though we all have a longing for it. Think about what we write on people's tombstones: Here rests so-and-so. Rest in peace. We see the words *rest* and *peace* everywhere in our cemeteries. We don't read much about net worth, fitness, and fame there. We humans share an inbuilt longing for peace. What would it be like if we could access that now and bring it to the way we work?

All our thoughts and feelings, the content of our experience, happen within a context. That context we can see as awareness. We have called it the sky. The sky is impartial, is empty, and at the same time encompasses all our clouds. It's hard to describe the context that we are, because we are looking from this context. We can use words like presence, unconditional love, peace, and joy to point to it, and yet that still doesn't do it justice. It is beyond all experiences and words, notices all experiences and words, and consists of all experiences and words. Another word for that may be reality. Being at one with reality, we no longer oppose anything, yet we contain everything at the same time. Who we truly are is a mystery that may be the greatest mystery we ever meet.

Have you ever been really sad? Did you notice that besides being really sad, there was also a place in you that noticed the sadness? Maybe you had a good cry and you felt some lightness in you. We can see this lightness as a pointer to who we are. In the Tao is my favorite quote of all time: "Knowing constancy is insight, not knowing constancy leads to disaster." What is constant then? What is constant cannot be described. We can approach it by being present in the here and now and by becoming supremely disinterested in all of the content of our experience without rejecting any of it. We embrace any discomfort and don't set up camp in any pleasure. We are with the pleasure and pain without becoming it. We are the unchanging sky that contains it all. Resting as the sky gives us a foundation that outlives all our thoughts and feelings. Even a thought about possible destruction of our planet is seen as just a thought, albeit a painful one. From presence, we stay grounded in presence and simply let the thought be what it is.

That doesn't mean we don't do anything about the challenges of our time. On the contrary. We are fully engaged, without getting lost in the experience. We are not expecting that finding resolution will give us lasting peace. Imagine that tomorrow you found a solution for climate change and all other problems you can think of. Would you be at peace? Maybe for a moment. And before you knew it, there would be an itch, a trigger, a thought, that demanded your attention again.

When we are aware that we are the peace we have been looking for everywhere outside of us, our thinking relaxes. No longer do we frantically need to solve our external world to get peace inside. We free up our thinking to focus on reality as it is, including climate change. Being conscious that we *are* peace, we become better equipped to work with the challenges of our time, as we no longer divert precious time and attention to finding peace for ourselves. We already have it. As soon as we realize our own peace, our innate constancy, we see it in everyone around us, also in others who haven't woken up to their inner peace yet.

Our crocodiles read this and may think: Yes, but how do I get anything done now? I am too busy to be peaceful. And besides that, I feel stressed out now, not peaceful at all. This is understandable crocodilian talk; our crocodiles dread peace. They never want us to let our defenses down. They want us to keep striving, no matter what. In these moments, we can take a few deep breaths, come back to the here and now, become supremely disinterested in our experience, and rest as presence. We return to the silent place that is not suffering when we are, that is not excited when we are, that is just here—unchanging.

What would it be like to live and lead more and more from that unchanging place?

---

## Leadership Practice

*Ask yourself: On a scale from 1 to 10, how much are you at peace right now? What thoughts are telling you that you can't be at peace? Who would you be without these thoughts?*

*Give yourself permission to experience the peace that you are, if only for a few moments. What is it like? How do you approach the challenges of today from the peace that you are?*

## PRACTICE 68
## Letting Flow

A COACHING CONVERSATION, like any conversation, has a beginning, middle, and end to it. It's a particular kind of conversation, in that its intention is to help the coachee grow. Coachees grow as they access new insights. They discover new ways of seeing themselves, their aspirations and challenges and develop commitment to practice their new ways of being and doing. A great coaching conversation is a conversation where *ah-ha*s happen. How do we create a space that is conducive to ah-has?

Our crocodiles will try to control the conversation—pushing a formula, a structure, and an outcome, resisting life as it comes. Our crocodiles are too scared to be in the conversation as it flows. Or they give up altogether, become disengaged, or are unwilling to stay when things don't seem to go well.

What happens when we truly stay in the moment, with our coachee, in the conversation as it happens? Having had several coaching conversations, we may discover some patterns. These don't create a formula; they are simply pointers we can practice, like steps in a dance to get the hang of before we freestyle. We will know when we're ready to leave the pointers behind and start improvising.

How do we start our coaching conversation? First things first. We set the table and create a common context, starting with ourselves. We first set our inner table by being clear about our coaching intentions. We may ask ourselves: How present am I now, on a scale of 1 to 10? What is my intention for this conversation? Having energetically made ourselves ready, we welcome the coachee, help them feel at ease, and may talk a bit about the purpose of the conversation. We ask the coachee, especially if it's our first coaching conversation: Are you willing to be coached by me? We establish an explicit coaching contract. If the coachee doesn't give us permission to coach them, there can be no coaching. We only coach those who have explicitly asked for it. That is part of the safety we provide as coaches. No safety, no real coaching.

You have probably heard about the energetic flow of *forming, storming, norming, performing, and mourning.* We are now at the "forming" stage and shouldn't rush past it. We create a safe space where our mutual intentions become clear and explicit. Soon the question may arise: What do you want to be coached on? We help the coachee take a step back from their lives and set a learning intention for the coaching conversation.

The conversation flows as it will. We may continue with some "storming" questions. As a coach, we are not here to provide wise answers. We are here to question the answers the coachee believes they have, to help them become conscious of a bigger perspective. We let intuition guide us to find our questions. And importantly, we don't force anything. We LOVE—Letting Others Voluntarily Evolve. We may think that if the coachee doesn't get it they will get into big trouble. What we are really saying is that our self-image of being an effective coach is at risk. Giving in to this crocodilian "I should have the answer for you" hallucination, we likely deprive the coachee of a valuable learning opportunity. A crisis is a terrible thing to waste. Think of all the crises you have had in your life and what you have learned from them. Would you be who you are today if you had missed a single one of these upsets? If coachees are unwilling or unable to look, we let them stick with their interpretation—even if it's filled, from our point of view, with crocodilian biases. We never force anything.

Not pushing anything, we create a clear space that tends to create a vacuum effect. Nature abhors a vacuum. The coachee may feel magnetized by the silence and by not being pushed around—this may be a new experience for them—to look deeper. The coachee may be in the "storming" part of the flow for a while—letting the crocodilian stories surface and show their faces. Some of these faces may be quite polished. Yet all, when looked at deeply, will reveal their fear-based grimace. This is a time for deep self-honesty. And a time for deep self-love and self-acceptance. Only the coachee can draw their own conclusions. They will find this a lot easier to do when they hold themselves without judgment and with tons of love. As they do so, they access fresh ways of seeing. We are entering the "norming" part of the conversation.

We tend to learn most in difficult moments. In a coaching conversation, this may be the moment when the coachee feels stuck. We may simply hold up a mirror by being still, maybe saying, "What are you experiencing right now?" We help the coachee to stay as close as possible to their experience. The closer they stay, the more they will be able to receive the lessons from their discomfort.

We rest assured insights will come. We just don't know when. In a coaching conversation, once insights have been flowing and the coachee has started to see a new perspective, they may want to reflect on a broader pattern in their life. How is this insight part of my bigger journey? What are the bigger themes here? An insight starts to bloom in the coachee's being and reorients their inner landscape. The coachee starts to connect the dots. We call this the "performing" stage of the coaching conversation.

At the end of a coaching conversation, the "mourning" stage, we spend a few minutes gathering what we have learned, possibly making some commitments. How have you been growing through this conversation? What will you do to practice it? As coaches, we purposefully help bring the conversation to a close so that it will have lasting effect beyond the moment.

Forming, storming, norming, performing, mourning—they are steps in the dance of any conversation, including a coaching one. For each step there is some technique we can learn and master. Regardless of our technique, we can go on to the dance floor and be there with the coachee. In the end, it's very simple. We are present for them and there to be of service. That is our beat. The moves flow from that. We stay in flow as long as we are committed to presence and service. Of course, our crocodiles will have us trip up. No problem. The music of life continues. We find our feet, take a breath, and rejoin the dance. We enjoy the dance of coaching.

## Leadership Practice

Reflect on the coaching stages: forming, storming, norming, performing, mourning. What is your strong suit?

What stage is most uncomfortable to you? What would happen if you allowed yourself to let the stage you're most uncomfortable with simply happen through you, without forcing it?

# PRACTICE 69
## Emptying out Our Body Library

Our bodies may be our greatest truth tellers. They will tell us immediately—something feels good, or it doesn't. A stressful thought translates into a painful feeling. The area below our neck faithfully copies—and, it turns out, stores—our thoughts, feelings, and memories. Our body never lies. It will tell us what we need to give attention to. We can ignore it, for sure. Somehow, what we ignore, what we suppress, stays in the body and becomes a tension area in our bodies—sometimes subtle, often quite painful.

Most of us have not been trained to pay close attention to our bodies and the information it stores for us, especially not the more painful feelings. We tend to repress them into our unconscious, into our bodies, our muscle tissue. We think this works, because we were never taught otherwise. Upon closer inspection, we may notice that ignoring our body's messages is costly. Most of us have many layers of contractions stored in our bodies from past upsets that we never addressed. These contractions may show up as increasing tightness in the belly, chest, throat, or shoulders; a feeling of imbalance between our right and left side; tight hips; or pain in our back, legs or feet. That's the bad news.

The good news is that we can work with our areas of contraction, not only to relax them, but also to glean valuable insights stored in them that can help us see ourselves and our challenges differently.

Let me give you an example. As I go through it, I invite you to do a similar process with yourself. Even if you do it a little bit, you may access some insights.

When I am relaxed, my body feels quite open. Triggered by a stressful event, some predictable places in my body tense up, especially on my right side—my shoulder, the right side of my lower belly, and my right hip. Even the right side of my face feels tight. You may notice something similar. The tension in my lower belly tends to be strongest. I can ask this part, like I would an innocent child: What is it that you would like me to do about the current upset? Spending a bit of time with my belly, I sense hopelessness stored there and also a need to react immediately. The sensation reminds me of how I felt as a child at times. This younger Hylke learned that he had to reestablish stability by pleasing people and conforming to what he believed were their expectations. And don't wait. Do it fast. Put everything else on hold. Fix it now, quickly! This same please-them-now energy still lives in my body. What does this child-energy want me to do about an upset I currently face? Apply the same kind of please-them-now, fix-it-now approach. When I give in to this energy, my options feel rather limited. I actually *become* the upset, rather than *having* an upset.

Ask yourself, if you like, what part of your body contracts when you have an upset. Where do you usually feel tension? Think of an upset you may be facing and look at it from the perspective of that contraction. Imagine drawing eyes on that part of your body. What do you notice? How does the contraction see the current upset? How does it want you to react? Chances are its repertoire of suggested thoughts, feelings, and actions is quite narrow, yet quite familiar to you. Take a moment to reflect what the impact will be on yourself, your relationships, and your effectiveness if you give in to the reactions suggested by this contracted energy.

In my case, I'd feel more stressed, as I would act out of integrity: I would undermine my relationships, and while I may possibly have some short-term success, longer term I am shooting myself in the foot by taking shortcuts now that will cost me later.

The localization of the contraction is a key to healing it. The remedy for many contractions is to be present to the contraction, exactly where it is in the body. Simply be with it as a mother would be with a child. It's important to be still with it. Yes, I know this is the last thing that the contraction wants. It wants you to *act out* rather than letting the energy *empty out*. It will naturally empty out as you spend a little time and attention with the contraction. You can even bring your sense of awareness, as a light, to the center of the contraction and let the awareness expand, radiate out, throughout the contraction. We are not pushing the contraction out—this would create another contraction. We're simply bringing awareness to it and letting it play out, just like we'd hold a crying baby. Eventually, they do go to sleep.

As the contraction relaxes, we relax also. We may notice some heart and mind space opening up. We may find ourselves feeling more creative, rather than reactive, in the face of the upset. We use the upset as a setup for our learning. We are choosing a different way than the child knew. As we choose a wiser, more compassionate way, we teach ourselves, and that part of our nervous system that may have been contracted for decades, a new way. Seeing our old, difficult memories with fresh awareness is the beginning of the end of their power over us. As they move from subject to object, we become able to look at them objectively, as not ours. They are not ours, they are simply an old habitual energy we learned to be in, often a long time ago. Who we are, the ground of our being, never changed. It is simply that we wore this energy impression, pretending we were it, thinking that this is what life feels like, not realizing there are many other ways to experience reality.

From this vantage point, noticing a contraction in our body becomes an act of empowerment. We empower ourselves by seeing which limiting beliefs our bodies had stored for us and by letting them go. We use our body's contractions to free ourselves from our limiting impressions. We use our body's contractions to birth ourselves anew.

This is not an event; this is an ongoing practice for most of us. It's like having many children. We can be with them, take care of them, help them grow up, and eventually leave the house.

---

## Leadership Practice

*Where in the body do you feel a contraction often? Rest your attention on the part of the body where the contraction is the strongest.*

*Now take a few deep conscious breaths into the belly.*

*If the contraction had full control over you, what would it want you to do? If you gave in to this reaction, what would be the impact on yourself (I), your relationships (We), and your effectiveness (It)?*

*Now bring some awareness to this contraction. Simply be with it. Allow it to open in its time. What becomes possible for you with this contraction releasing? Which new ways of seeing and acting do you see? What may be the impact of this on the I, We, and It?*

# PRACTICE 70
## Make it Practical

$P$RACTICE IS A bridge between insight and reality. Have you ever had a great insight, only to go back to the groove of your day-to-day without having changed a thing? Still, in the back of your mind you remember what you now know, but you operate as if nothing has happened. It takes commitment to live and lead from our highest truth. We can make that commitment purely on an energetic, intention basis—for example, committing to be truthful, present, and loving. We can also do so on a practical level. Committing to a few small things to do differently in our day can make a world of difference in our growth journey. We let ourselves know that we are now on a new path and that it's important enough for us to spend time and attention on it.

You decide what your practice is. No one can prescribe this for you. At the end of a coaching session, I tend to ask: How are you growing? And: How will you practice your insight? Practices I have used myself include meditation, taking a walk, qi gong, taking a moment before each meeting to check in with myself and others, taking a few deep conscious breaths into my belly every hour, taking breaks every ninety minutes, repeating a mantra to myself, doing a beginning-of-day intention setting and an after-the-day-is-over-after-action-review on my from-tos (the mindset shifts that I commit to), checking in with my feelings, reminding myself of my intentions, stretching, going to the gym, singing, speaking with a counselor or friend...and the list goes on.

My crocodile resists my doing any practice. It wants me to continue and stay busy with what I was doing already. Breaking my routine is out of the question for my crocodile. That would be too dangerous. As a practice to start my practice and overcome crocodilian resistance, I ask myself: Who is talking now, the owl or the crocodile? Of course, I know it's my crocodile. My wise owl is so happy that I spend a little bit of time with myself, to connect more deeply with who I really am.

Being in the practice, we often find it's not so bad at all. It can be deeply energizing. Plus, there is something that happens in us when we follow through on our commitments to ourselves. It reinforces our sense of dignity. Practice is a way of telling ourselves that we are worth it to be taken care of. We are worth it to be taken care of as the beautiful instrument of presence, truth, and love that we are. Our crocodiles have us run ragged. In our society we have put a premium on constantly being busy, never stopping. We are always in a rush to the next thing if we let our crocodile drive our agenda. Conversely, our wise self asks: Would you like to spend some time, just with me?

From the owl's perspective, we appreciate that applying new insights into our life, breaking habits, takes time. Most habits have been with us for our entire lives. Wouldn't it be reckless to assume we'd change just by having one insight or by having one thought about it? Whole parts of our nervous system—how we think about something, how we sense, how we interact, how we take action—may need to adjust. This takes time. Doing some practice, we integrate, we bring together the different pieces of our nervous system into a newly coherent whole. With practice we massage the stiffness out of our being.

In some instances, a changeover does take place in a split second. Something in us breaks open and never really closes again. Even then we may still want to practice. I find that practice gives me joy. It's an anchor point in the day for me to go sit down in my meditation area every morning. It's become as routine as brushing my teeth; it happens as if on autopilot. Sitting down, I experience the full gamut of human emotions. And I can't remember a single time that I regretted spending some time in meditation. It's always helped me in some way.

How will you practice your insights? Do something that fits with you, something that energizes you, that you may look forward to. Make it fun, maybe even playful. It doesn't so much matter what it is. What matters is that you dedicate time and attention to your growth. Paying conscious attention to your growth nourishes it.

Beware of any crocodiles that may evaluate how well you are doing the practice and how much impact you are getting, and that fret about what you should be accomplishing. Instead of doing the practice, they may try to dissuade you from doing any practice at all. Noticing this self-talk, simply stop and ask yourself: Who is talking now, the owl or the crocodile? Oh, our little friend never really rests, does he now? We look at him with kind eyes and do our practice anyway.

---

## Leadership Practice

*Reflect on a few insights you have had about yourself recently. What is one simple practice you could do to embody your insight more? Do this practice seven times this week and see what happens.*

*What practices do you have that have become habits? What does it feel like when a practice that you are doing consistently crosses the threshold to become a new habit?*

# PART 8

## Being Agents of Love

## PRACTICE 71
## What Is Your Meta-Story?

THERE YOU ARE in a meeting. There you are at the computer doing your email. There you are having breakfast. There you are working out. There you are taking care of the children. We find ourselves at so many stations in any one given day. Is there an overarching story that is always true about you, no matter where you are and what you are doing? If you found your story, what would the impact be on yourself and the people around you of you being committed to that story? Of you living that story to the fullest?

Our crocodile does have a powerful story about us—it tells us that we need to protect ourselves and work for our survival. *Punto e basta*—that's it. From there we may spin other stories—all derived from the crocodilian meta-story that we need to protect our ego at all cost—like: I am all about doing it perfectly, being better than you, being a nobody, pleasing you, making me right and you wrong, worrying all the time, having all the answers, rescuing others, being the Wise One, and being the Special One.

What would be a story that is true about you, no matter what is happening, coming from your highest self? No one can tell you. What is your highest truth about yourself? What do you know deep down has always been true about you? Maybe you sense you are about being truthful and unconditionally loving. Or maybe you sense you are in essence a deep stillness that connects us all. Maybe you sense an aspect about you that's always true, that's about being open and willing to learn. Or maybe you love helping others, no matter what. What is always true about you?

Knowing what's always true about us is empowering. We can remind ourselves to come back to that truth, no matter what situation we're in. Imagine we'd found that we're really about being deeply loving, no matter what. How would reminding ourselves of this change the energy we bring to a conflict? To a new team member? To someone we walk by on the street? To the person we email? To a person that cuts us off in traffic?

Being committed to our highest truth and living it day by day is a task and a journey. We task ourselves to bring the energy of our highest truth to every moment. And we are open to the journey of finding out what that looks like and what the impact will be. We trust our highest truth to lead the way.

And as we live that, we may find out a deeper truth about ourselves that lies underneath the truth we had realized so far. It's like the woodcarver who, by sheer attention to the wood, starts to discover the even more beautiful shapes that are hidden below the surface. Living our highest truth, we chip away at our illusions and start seeing truth about ourselves that we otherwise wouldn't. We start seeing what our truth is about. And we start to recognize the hallucinations that were buried in our earlier understanding.

We shouldn't underestimate the power of one person living their highest truth. Think of all that a little guy like Gandhi was able to put in motion, in large part because of his commitment to stay true to his nonchanging values: nonviolence and truth. We don't exist independently. We exist interdependently, always part of a larger system, be it our company, our team, our friends, our family, our neighbors, our town, our nation, our world, and so on. That system changes even if only one person changes. The rest of the system will adjust.

Imagine what may become possible for the people you care about if you commit to living your highest truth more fully. What may become possible for you? What awareness and choices may that elicit in others? Now imagine yourself staying committed to your highest truth, even if the system doesn't seem to care, or reacts negatively. How will you feel? What may be the longer-term impact of that? How may it help you and the system grow over time?

Being a leader is a mindset much more than a role. We can choose to be leaders of ourselves by staying committed to our highest truth and lead ourselves, guided by the compass of our highest truth, through life's ups and downs. We learn to be rooted in and delight in our highest truth.

It's such a great friend to have around. We bring that friend anywhere. Our friend may inspire others to find their inner friend, their highest truth.

Living our truth, we inspire the energy of *satsang*, from Sanskrit, meaning "gathering in truth." We bring the energy of truth wherever we go. That way, we're always in good company. This energy creates an atmosphere that invites self-reflection and openness.

Now, watch our little crocodile with this. We're not going to fall for its hallucinatory expectation that people will automatically open up because we are opening up. We are simply contributing to the many causes and conditions that help people around us make their own choices. Their choices are not up to us. What is up to us is that we stay committed to our highest truth, no matter what.

***

## Leadership Practice

*Reflect for a moment. What is the highest truth you have realized about yourself? What is always true about you? What would it be to live that truth more in every moment of the next twenty-four hours? Then what would become possible for you?*

## PRACTICE 72
### The First Choice in Every Moment

GROWTH IS NOT glamorous. Well, sometimes it may be, for example when we're having a big, new insight or we are seeing the impact our new mindset has on how we and others feel and act. However, 99.9 percent of the time growth happens without fanfare. If we want to inspire others to grow by being a role model, we need to be a role model, especially when they are not watching us.

Each moment we stand at a crossroads—will I take the high road or the well-trodden path that my crocodile wants me to revert back to? Each of these micro-choices, one micro-moment at a time, makes a life. What will my choice be in this moment?

I was recently on a conference call just now to discuss a possible new team development engagement with a client. I hadn't slept super well the night before and felt a bit sluggish. My crocodiles were saying: You are not going to be creative enough to have this conversation! And also, go for the close. You need to make sure your business keeps growing. Hearing these voices, I felt discouraged. Yikes, with this much crocodile screaming in my head, how could I ever have a good conversation?

Something dawned on me: Who was talking now? The owl or the crocodile? It turned out that my crocodile, impersonating a wise owl, was judging me for having crocodilian thoughts. Clever crocodile; it will do anything it can to keep us under its control. If putting myself down doesn't work, then putting myself down for putting myself down might do the job!

I wish I could tell you my crocodiles just gave up the fight and went home. They didn't. They started saying things like: "See, even the fact that you are thinking about this has you not being present to this moment. You are failing!" and "You are not enlightened enough to serve this client." Our crocodiles are stubborn. Even with them on the scene, we still can make another choice—or, I should say, especially when they are on the scene, we need to make another choice.

While my crocodiles were performing their drama, there was another part in me that watched it dispassionately. I chose to connect to this saner, balcony part and distance myself from the crocodilian drama. Being on the balcony, I set a micro-intention for myself: Let me be of service here, no matter what. I intend to be loving and give my best. Now. And now. And now.

Somehow, the conversation with the client flowed. We got to a place of understanding, even developed a proposal together for how we could help the team become bolder. Interestingly, that was exactly what I was learning about myself: how to boldly stand up to the crocodiles and take a stand for my highest self.

I have noticed that these moments of boldness become new memories that help me be bolder next time. I remember that it was possible to choose differently. And I remember the fulfillment I felt being in integrity with myself. Something in us celebrates every micro-moment we take a stand for truth.

Choosing to stand for truth requires that we listen to the space that lies beyond our crocodilian chatter. Sometimes we may have twenty different crocodilian radio stations blaring in our head at the same time. That can feel confusing and overwhelming. In these moments, we can remember that reality is much simpler than our crocodiles make it out to be. It always starts with us making a choice: Where do we place our attention now? Do we listen to our crocodiles? Or do we pause and check in with our highest truth? It's really that simple. The crocodile will say, "Yes, but you need to listen to me, I have valuable information for you." Yes, that may be so. And we know we can't make sense of anything when we are listening from fearful crocodile consciousness. What is the highest truth that we are committed to? Looking from that highest truth—maybe it's unconditional love, or being present or at peace—what do we realize now? What is this moment about? What are our choices?

We resolve to stay awake and not let ourselves be hypnotized by the plethora of crocodilian voices. That's the first choice we make in every moment. All the other choices stem from that one.

Imagine your life for the next ten years. What will become possible for you when you choose to make moment-to-moment choices coming from your highest truth? Now contrast this path with staying on the road of the crocodilian slumber party.

Which way do you choose to go now?

---

## Leadership Practice

*In this moment, notice the choice you have. Imagine for a moment you decide to go the crocodilian route. Visualize yourself really taking this path. What will be the impact on your sense of fulfillment (I), your relationships (We), and your effectiveness (It)?*

*What would it be like if you chose to approach this moment from your highest truth? See yourself following this path and feel deeply what comes up. What will be the impact of that on your I, We, and It?*

# PRACTICE 73
## Choose Your Word

A WORD CAN make a world of difference. Consider just how powerful words are. Helen Keller's life can teach us about this. She became deaf-blind at nineteen months old when she contracted a disease that doctors were unable to diagnose, and lived without any relationship to words almost until the age of seven. Take a moment to imagine what it would be like if you became deaf and blind as an infant. How would you relate to the world then? How would you feel?

You wouldn't be able to hear or see anything. You'd be in total darkness, and in a deep silence. You'd still notice images and feelings. You'd be able to smell, taste, and touch. But how would you make sense of your experience if you hadn't heard or seen a single word? How would you relate to others then? This was one of the first things Anne Sullivan, Helen's tutor, helped her with—how to make sense of her world and communicate with others. She did this by spelling words in Helen's hand. For a while, Helen didn't comprehend what was happening. Why was this woman touching her hand so much? Why was she repeating the same movements over and over? Weeks went by and then, one day, as Anne was spelling w-a-t-e-r in Helen's hand while holding her other hand underneath a running faucet, Helen grasped the meaning of what Anne was showing her. She comprehended that the motions of Anne's fingers had something to do with the substance she was feeling in her other hand. Helen wrote in her autobiography:

*"I stood still, my whole attention fixed upon the motions of her fingers. Suddenly I felt a misty consciousness as of something forgotten—a thrill of returning thought; and somehow the mystery of language was revealed to me. I knew then that w-a-t-e-r meant the wonderful cool something that was*

*flowing over my hand. The living word awakened my soul, gave it light, hope, set it free!"*

We learn to relate to our world through language when we are very young. Language helps us make sense. Language helps us navigate our lives. With language, we learn to make distinctions, understand, even dream. With language, we write the stories of our lives. "The mystery of language" helps us relate to the mystery of our lives. Language helps us discern.

We use the discerning quality of language to help us grow and serve others. We use language to name our crocodiles and let go of our unconscious, fear-based self-talk. We learn we have the capacity to place our time and attention on our highest truth by having the words to speak about it. We use words to imprint questions, insights, and choices in our being so we can consciously work with them. Without words, we'd be to a large extent rudderless. Words give us agency. They help us discern this from that. Without this ability to cognate we would not be able to make choices. Even our dreams include words, besides images we sometimes later remember in words.

In our growth journey, we'll have many moments where words make a difference. We remember in the heat of the moment that we want to be honest and kind, or to take it easy, and one day at a time. We may remember about the crocodile and the owl, and to redirect our attention from the crocodile to the owl. With words, we help to steer the ship of our inner selves by changing our inner narrative, our self-talk.

Hearing certain words, we have an almost instantaneous visceral response. Think of a word like "love," or "birth," or "death." Some words stir quite a bit of movement in us.

We can use the power of words by consciously selecting a few to guide our growth journeys. We call these words *language markers*. They are like markers on a trail. They help us out when we need a little nudge or some direction. How am I to respond here? Having simple language markers can help us stay the course and not get lost in the crocodilian labyrinth.

Some of my favorite language markers include: Is this true? Who is talking now, the owl or the crocodile? How am I growing? and How can I respond from my highest truth now? They have become reliable guides to traverse many a challenging crocodilian moment.

Language markers become even more powerful when they become shared. I have seen teams, whole organizations, nations, and even the world, make significant changes motivated by a few powerful language markers. One team decided to adopt *Courage over comfort* as their language marker. In the United States, *Be safe* has become a common way of saying goodbye after 9/11, reminding us to stay vigilant. And within companies, words like *growth mindset* are motivating people to stay open to new possibilities.

Take a moment and ask yourself: What is a word, or a few words that have meaning for you and can help you stay on your path? The living word gave Helen's soul *"light, hope, set it free!"* How can words help you on your path today?

---

## Leadership Practice

*Think of your most significant growth edges. What crocodiles have the greatest grip on you? Which owl mindsets would you like to practice and cultivate instead of the crocodilian reactivity?*

*What are a few words, a language marker, that can remind you to choose your owl path, especially when you are under stress?*

Going to church on Sunday mornings, having coffee and cake afterwards, and sharing meals were some of my favorite rituals as a kid. I also loved my music lessons and biking to high school with my friend alongside a Rembrandt-like river. I didn't realize it at the time, but now, looking back, I recognize a quiet power in these rituals. They interrupted the regular flow of the week as we made space for something else: for deep conversation over coffee and cake; for artistic expression during music lessons; and for reflecting with my friend, peddling through the fields, on what this life is all about.

Shared rituals, especially if we hold them with intention, can become places where we take a step back together. It's balcony time for us. We take a look, take stock, reflect, and share what we see. We pause what we are doing and pay attention to something else than what regularly absorbs us. We interrupt the momentum of our lives.

These days, one of my favorite rituals is the check-in: a sequential monologue, where each in turn speaks their truth about a few questions we agree on beforehand. These questions include: How are you feeling? How are you growing? and What is your intention for this meeting? The power of this ritual is in part in what we *don't* do. We don't interrupt or respond in any other way than saying "Thank you" after each share. My crocodile still sometimes thinks this is a colossal waste of time: all this listening...When are we going to get something done? Actually, a lot gets done. We speak our truths and share them with each other. Each person who speaks contributes to the fabric of safety and relatedness. One by one, we build connection. Also, we are there to receive what people are saying. It's liberating to speak when we know that the person we are speaking to will not try to solve our issue for us. It makes it easier to speak our truth, as we are no longer concerned about it being an imposition on the other. We are speaking our truth to share it, not to have others take it up as their homework to do.

Shared rituals like check-ins gain power by doing them repeatedly. We come to rely on them. For example, we know that whatever happens in our day, we will have a check-in where we can share and connect with each other. And with practice, we learn to use the ritual more skillfully and easily.

Rituals can be helpful tools when we are on a growth journey together. We choose them deliberately. Which rituals will we choose that best capture the shift in mindsets and behaviors we are aspiring to? Which rituals feel closest to home and are most natural to us?

One ritual my partner and I have is that we hold hands for a moment in stillness before sharing our meals together. I have come to rely on this custom. I sit down and automatically my hand reaches for his and I become quiet for a moment. Rituals help us to reorient ourselves to the things we value most.

Our crocodiles hold us hostage in plenty of unconscious rituals when we let them: overworking, not taking breaks, checking emails obsessively, procrastinating, checking up on others to make sure we're ok, always asking what's wrong, giving advice, over-preparing, etc. Our crocodiles are creative habit builders.

Choosing our rituals consciously, rather than letting the crocodile define them, is our way of saying to life and to each other: I value our shared priorities and I am committed to dedicating time and attention to them. Rituals take dedication. We choose them. As we choose them they choose us, like old friends that are happy to see us again. Powerful rituals nourish us. Think of great workouts, hikes, or retreats you have done. Maybe you weren't sure about doing them before you got started and then you were so happy that you did it anyway. They invigorate us. They help us connect more deeply to who we are and to each other.

What is a ritual you are already doing? What if you gave this ritual even a little bit more time, attention, and appreciation, like a good friend? What is a new ritual you may want to explore together with others?

One caveat: Rituals are acts of volition, not of coercion. A ritual becomes more powerful when we feel just as free to participate as to pass.

Then a ritual becomes a symbol of the sky of awareness, of the being that we are. The sky doesn't force anyone. Yet there is a natural rhythm to the goings-on in the sky. The clouds appear in some sort of unfathomable harmony. We bring this freedom and the harmony into our rituals by making clear agreements about what our intentions are and the process that we will follow, and by giving people the explicit option to not participate.

Rituals invite us to connect to ourselves and each other. What ritual would you like to invite yourself into today?

---

## Leadership Practice

*What growth in mindsets and behaviors do you aspire to in a community you are part of, be it your family and friends, your team at work, your chosen charity, or any other group you are part of?*

*What is a ritual you can continue or start that will support your growing together?*

# PRACTICE 75
## Self-Giving

NATURE GIVES, GIVES, and gives. Every morning, the sun rises and graces us with light. Rain feeds our crops. Darkness provides rest. Gravity gives us stability. Our bodies give to us nonstop: breathing, digesting, feeling, thinking, expressing. Our body gives itself to everything we engage in. Nature gives.

We are a part of nature. To be in harmony with it, we do as nature does. We give. That may be one reason why it feels good to give—to prepare a meal for someone, to say a kind word, to help someone cross the street, to support someone in a conversation, to help someone heal, to help get things done. It feels great to give. Giving of ourselves, we implicitly affirm how we are part of nature.

What we essentially have to give comes down to two words: time and attention. Time and attention are our two most valuable assets. What do we give our time and attention to? Have you noticed that whatever you give attention to becomes more vivid, more alive in your experience? So, what is it that you wish to be more alive in your experience? Having something that is alive in our experience guides us. When we give ourselves to the ground of our being, our essence, this becomes more alive in our experience. The more time we spend with a friend, the better we get to know them. The more time and attention we spend with our essence, the more familiar it becomes to us. Our essence lights up in us. With practice, it becomes a guiding light in our day.

What we give attention to gives back to us. The more we give ourselves to presence, the more we unite with it, the more it starts to fill us up, and the more it gives us the foundation from which we can engage with life. When we give ourselves to our true selves, our true self comes and greets us. It comes to our help. It is here to comfort us, to strengthen us, to delight us.

The more we give ourselves to our true selves, the more we will feel called to give to others. We want to share our beautiful experience with others. Great art comes from this. Also, constructive, compassionate words and insights come from this place. We become more open to listen to others, as we become more firmly grounded in the openness that presence provides us with. We become decisive and firm, as presence provides us with the ground to stand on and the intuitive insights to guide us.

What do you want to give your time and attention to today? Our crocodile has a very full agenda for us. Our fear-based conditioning wants us to give all our time and attention to fear-based thinking and actions, worrying, taking shortcuts, pleasing others and judging them when they don't comply with our expectations of them, trying to micromanage, validating our rigid viewpoints, dominating and rescuing others, and making ourselves the center of others' attention by being the Sapient One and the Special One. The crocodile has umpteen strategies to keep us busy. Each strategy is a time sink—a bottomless pit. We can never do enough and never be enough to complete our crocodilian agenda. We'll always be behind, feel harried, and never really be effective. How could we be? We are acting based on hallucination, rather than reality.

Giving our time and attention to what is true—starting with what is true about ourselves, our essence, unconditional love, presence, peace— we can't help but share that with others. Stepping more and more into our true selves, we share that energy with others, instead of imposing our crocodilian agenda of "all about me" on them. We are simply here. We extend that here-ness to others.

Most of us have breakfast in the morning, in part to energize ourselves for the new day. What would it be like if we spent some time each day replenishing ourselves by giving ourselves to presence? Imagine the strength, the compassion, the insight that we may find in the stillness of our being. Like drinking water throughout the day, we can come back to presence, moment by moment, throughout our day. Presence will always be here to nourish us.

## Leadership Practice

*What does your crocodile want you to give your time and attention to today? What does the crocodile do to make sure you focus on those things?*


*What do you choose to give your time and attention to? What do you imagine your day will look like when you truly give your time and attention to your intention?*

# PRACTICE 76
## Unconditional Gratitude as True Self-Affirmation

WHAT ARE YOU grateful for in your journey? What are you grateful for in your life? Gratitude is a mindset we learn early on. "Say thank you to your aunt and uncle," our parents may have said to us. "Thank you," may be among our most powerful words, alongside love, truth, peace, and joy. Thank you for today. Thank you for this moment. Thank you for this body. Thank you for this mind. Thank you for this work. Thank you for this food. Thank you for this friend. Thank you for awareness. Thank you for insight. Thank you for being able to give thanks.

Something in us unlocks when we say thank you and we mean it. We lose rigidity and resistance and we open to life as it is. And we don't stop there. Being in gratitude, we don't only open to life; we also say what we appreciate about it. We bow to life. We realize how perfect this moment is, even if it didn't quite fit our expectations.

I was on a call just now with my credit card company for about one hour. It was because of a transaction that was being disputed. I could feel my inner contraction. "No, I don't want to be here. This should not be happening," screamed my crocodile. From this contracted place I wanted to berate the person I was speaking with, for what my crocodile thought were very good reasons. Weren't they incompetent, untrustworthy, unreliable, and shortsighted for not giving me the service I wanted in the time I wanted it to happen?!

Thankfully, I was awake to another place in me, a deeper human place, that could see beyond my expectations of what I thought should happen into the power of the present moment. Yes, it did entail my taking some deep breaths. I chose to open a bit more. I relaxed. I started having a real conversation with the credit card representative I had been speaking with. His name turned out to be Abhishek, which means "coronation" in his native language. Something in me lit up when I heard this. What might this moment be teaching me was a question I heard from a deeper, more intuitive place. What can I be thankful for now? How is this moment with Abhishek affirming who I really am and who he really is? How is this moment crowning both of us? While Abhishek and I were on hold, waiting to reach a contact person at the merchant we needed to speak to in order to get the transaction completed, we got a bit deeper into the conversation. He told me he came from the foothills in India. That he was an artist. And that his favorite book was called *The City of Joy*. "You know," he said, "there are these people living in shantytowns in Calcutta. And with new modern high-rises going up all around them, these people just go about their day, being in joy and peace with each other. They remain unaffected by what's happening around them. They live in a constant state of joy." I listened to his words. The completion of my transaction started to feel less all-consuming. A broader perspective dawned. If these people could be joyous living in squalor, could I find joy being here, in my cozy home, speaking to a wonderful fellow human being, getting some new furniture? No question about it.

After we hung up the phone, I started wondering how I could be more like the people in the city of joy Abhishek was describing. How would it be if I moved from conditional gratitude to unconditional gratitude? What would that be like? Being unconditionally grateful, I would greet every moment, no matter what's in it, with openness and appreciation. Every moment would be a gift of which I'd be the grateful recipient. Come to think of it, being unconditionally grateful, we are aligning ourselves, we are restoring ourselves to our essence, the pure sky of presence, love, peace, and joy that knows no conditions, embraces everything, and includes everything because it is everything. Being grateful, we open to life and life opens to us. No longer weighed down by our expectations of what should be, we free ourselves to be fully with what is. We waste no more precious time and attention arguing with life. We accept it, we open to it, we appreciate it. We simply say thanks.

A conversation, whatever the other person may be saying to us, simply becomes an opportunity for us to extend gratitude. We are grateful for all that we are learning, for being together, for being alive now. This doesn't mean we agree with the other. We are equally grateful for the thoughts that come through them as the thoughts that come through us. With gratitude, our sight, once clouded, clears up enough for us to see reality. We see what is. With that clarity, we make more informed choices. *Choices based in gratitude are choices based in reality. Choices based in resistance and judgment are choices based in hallucinations.* If I had given in to my crocodilian projections, I would have had a short, scolding exchange with some person from the credit card company. I would have never gotten to know Abhishek or *The City of Joy*. I would have left the conversation stressed out, and likely my transaction wouldn't have gone through. I would have lost out on all fronts.

With gratitude, we embrace what is. Gratitude is courageous. It requires that instead of shrinking from life and shirking our responsibilities, we open to life, no matter what presents itself. Being grateful, we open ourselves to the infinite strength of the universe that comes through all of us. Being grateful, we become resourceful, as we appreciate the resources that are right here, right now, coming through us and the other, in this present moment.

---

## Leadership Practice

*In this moment, think of five things you are grateful for. Now think of another five things you are grateful for, and include things you don't like.*

*How would it be if you decided to become unconditionally grateful in every moment? Then what would become possible for you?*

*What ritual could you adopt that can help you return to gratitude more easily?*

# PRACTICE 77
## Stillness

No matter what is going on in our world, we can always come back to the silence underneath it all. Our thoughts and emotions tend to be demanding. They want us to do or be something. What do I need to do about this? What do I need to say? How can I feel better? How can I keep this good feeling? The silence underneath makes no such demands. It simply is. It doesn't argue. It doesn't try to feel better. It simply rests in itself.

The silence underneath it all may be the most important leadership competency we ever develop. Grounded in silence, we become unflinching. We are no longer tossed around by the ups and downs of life, as we have anchored in something that holds the ups and downs, something that is constant.

We can't develop this silence. It is already here. We simply allow ourselves to become aware of the silence in our being that underlies it all, like the sky that holds all the clouds in the sky without being attached to any of them.

This silence can appear inaccessible, particularly when we are in the midst of an emotional upheaval with our mental and emotional chatter at storm level. Our head is spinning and we feel ungrounded. Where is the silence of our being then? Of course, it hasn't gone anywhere. It is simply here. It's up to us to return our time and attention to it. Our mental and emotional system has a tendency to intoxicate us, especially in reactive crocodilian mode. In the grip of crocodilian hallucination, we believe our problems to be true and insurmountable, and we become identified, we become one, with the upheaval in our energy. We believe ourselves to be a cloud, as opposed to remembering that, in essence, we are the sky that is observing it all.

There is a taboo on resting as the sky. Aren't we supposed to be engaged, lean in, and always be busy? Resting as the sky is irresponsible, even lazy, argues our crocodile. We have become so enamored with our conditioned thinking that we have become identified with it. As may happen when we fall in love with someone and make them our whole life, we have been forgetting who we are.

Silence doesn't mind at all; it is always here, no matter what crocodilian hallucination we may be lost in for the moment. Asking the question, "Is this thought absolutely true?" can bring us back to reality. It interrupts the crocodilian momentum. It stops us in our tracks. We pause. In that pause, a greater truth reveals itself. We realize that underneath all our thinking and feeling, there is a sense of foundational okay-ness. The clouds part and the sun of our being shines through it, and we feel the warmth of being, at home in our constancy.

Pausing at the space between our out- and in-breath provides another crack in the crocodilian story. Our breathing, like our thoughts, keeps going. And in the midst of our breathing, we find these moments of stillness where the body just rests. That space between the exhale and inhale is one powerful gate into the silence that we are.

Yet another way to connect to our innate silence is by drawing our attention to the space behind our head and our heart. For most of us, our crocodiles want to always move forward and focus on what's ahead of us, both figuratively and literally. We place our attention on our devices, our screens, what we are doing with our hands, and what we are seeing. We are conditioned to place our attention in front of us. Placing our attention gently on the space behind us, behind our head and heart, helps to connect to another dimension of our being. Imagine you could rest in the space behind you. What would that be like? Take a moment and try it out now. Rest in the space behind you. Trust it. You may find it unfamiliar, maybe even empty or boring, as your mind may not have occupied and done much with this space before. Rest in this empty house. This house is another gateway into the silence that we are.

Silence, in the meantime, is just here. It doesn't need a technique to be here. It is simply here. Techniques like consciously focusing our attention on the space between our breaths, or on the space behind our head and heart, can make the silence of our being more a lived experience.

Giving ourselves to this silence, we discover it is vast, wise, deep, and caring. It places no conditions on us and yet is always here for us. We can trust it. We can rest in it. We can even give our attention to it with reverence, standing in awe at the gate of the essence of our being.

This silence is not static. It is light and dynamic. Motivation and inspiration spring from it. It fuels creativity, caring, and wisdom. Grounded in the stillness of our being, we know exactly what to do, and when to do it, in harmony with the all. From the silence, we simply notice our crocodilian thoughts and feelings, like children who are clamoring for our attention. All we really need to do is to remind these parts of ourselves that are not grounded yet that we are the silence, completely here, and accepting them as they mature and lose their reactivity. We don't identify with them. We simply rest as silence and patiently watch as our being is increasingly held and infused by the essence of what we are.

---

## Leadership Practice

*Notice the space between your inhale and exhale. Rest your attention there. What is it like to be at rest for a moment in between the activity of your breathing, thinking, and feeling? Now allow yourself to drop all technique. Simply be with yourself for a moment, without changing a thing about your experience. What are you noticing?*

*Enjoy this journey into the ground of your being, the stillness for which there are no words.*

# List of Practices

## Part 1: Exploring Foundational Growth Practices

## Part 2: Living and Growing from Intention

## Part 3: Facing Our Fears

21.  Working with Fear for Peace

22.  Standing on the Shoulders of Our Seven Fear Families

23.  Plenty of Love to Go Around—Taming the Scarcity Crocodile

24.  Daring to be Genuine—Taming the Abandonment Crocodile

25.  From Perfect Little Me to Purposefulness—Taming the Failure Crocodile

26.  The Heart of Discovery—Taming the Uncertainty Crocodile

27.  From Smokescreen into the Fire of Truth—Taming the Hurt Crocodile

28.  The Silence Underneath the Chaos—Taming the Complexity Crocodile

29.  Let "You" Be Temporary—Taming the Identity Crocodile

30.  Letting Fear Go, Letting Reality In

## Part 4: Enjoying Balance

31.  Finding Balance

32.  Yang Resolve

33.  Opening to Being a Yin Embrace

34.  From the Rocks into the River

35.  Clean Warmth or a Hot Mess?

36.  Sky-like Presence

37.  Doing Nothing

38.  Finding the Balance We Always Are

39.  Accepting Our Experience

40.  Joining Balance

## Part 5: Finding Truth

41.  True Freedom

42.  Spotting the Crocodilian Blockbuster Movies

# Acknowledgments

I AM GRATEFUL to be sharing this book with you. And I am grateful to all those who have been helping me in my journey and with this book.

Thank you, Jonelle Reynolds, for your showing me unconditional love and finding that in myself. Thank you, Adyashanti, for being and for your teachings, always taking me deeper. Thank you, Seymour Boorstein, for introducing me to the symbols and wisdom of the owl and the crocodile. Thank you, Byron Katie, for sharing the Work with all of us. Thank you, Jahon Brown, for showing me how truth and love are in the end the same. Thank you, Rick Gage, Sandra Baaijens, Mieke Kissing, Sava Riaskoff, and Isabella Steele for helping to edit this book. Thank you, Fiona Hallowell and your colleagues at Dover Publications, for your wise and caring refinements of the manuscript. Thank you, René Yoakum, for writing the foreword and being a role model of heart-based leadership to me and many. Thank you, Gaurav Bhatnagar and my former colleagues at Co-Creation Partners, for showing me how to really serve people and for introducing me to the Qs of coaching. Thank you, Fred Kofman, for helping me become a facilitator and for introducing me to Authentic Truth and many other wisdom tools. Thank you, Nicolas Blaiotta, for your unwavering support and compassion. Thank you, Mom and Dad, for always being there for me. Thank you, Nienke Schaap, Goska Sixma, Andre Oost, Renee Metty and Kaycee Bernier and my other colleagues at Growth Leaders Network and The Crocodile School, for being examples to me of the love we are. Thank you, Mieke Bouwens and Arthur Oostvogel for sharing your unconditional acceptance and kindness with me. Thank you to all my other friends, clients, former colleagues and everyone else I have ever met. Each of you has taught me more about what is true. You have helped me write this book.

Finally, thank you to all the teachers who, across history, have dedicated their lives to truth, often at great personal cost. Thank you for paving the way on which we walk.

# About the Author

HYLKE FABER'S MISSION is to realize his essence and help others do the same. He shares *Taming Your Crocodiles Practices* to help all of us, including himself, take the next step in our endless journey to become more of who we truly are.

Hylke Faber received his Bachelor's degree in Business Administration from the Netherlands' Nijenrode University and a Master of Arts in International Relations from Johns Hopkins University. He served as a Partner at Co-Creation Partners and Strategic Decisions Group and as a consultant at Axialent and Towers Perrin, supporting leaders across multiple industries globally on strategy, organization, and culture development programs. He is the author of the award-winning book *Taming Your Crocodiles: Unlearn Fear & Become a True Leader*, teaches the "Leader as Coach" courses at Columbia Business School and has contributed to *Harvard Business Review*. He is a facilitator and coach in Constancee, the leadership development company, and leads two coaching organizations, Growth Leaders Network and the Crocodile School. He lives in Seattle, Washington.

# Learn More

IF YOU WOULD like to read more about the owl and the crocodile, you may enjoy: *"Taming Your Crocodiles: Unlearn Fear & Become a True Leader."*

Do you want to learn together with others about taming your crocodiles and bringing them under the aegis of your wise, compassionate owl? Please connect with us at the Crocodile School, at www.thecrocodileschool.com.

Or maybe you are interested to apply this work in your organization? Please connect with us at Growth Leaders Network, at www.growthleadersnetwork.com.